Thomas Kilroy with his dog Mitzi at his home in Kilmaine, County Mayo

Across the Boundaries:

Talking about Thomas Kilroy

Across the Boundaries:
Talking about Thomas Kilroy

Edited by Guy Woodward

Carysfort Press

A Carysfort Press Book in association with Peter Lang
Across the Boundaries: Talking about Thomas Kilroy
Edited by Guy Woodward
First published in Ireland in 2014 as a paperback original by
Carysfort Press, 58 Woodfield, Scholarstown Road
Dublin 16, Ireland

ISBN 978-1-78874-807-0

©2014 Copyright remains with the authors

Typeset by Carysfort Press
Cover design by eprint limited

This book is published with the financial assistance of
The Arts Council (An Chomhairle Ealaíon) Dublin, Ireland

Caution: All rights reserved. No part of this book may be printed or reproduced or utilized in any form or by any electronic, mechanical, or other means, now known or hereafter invented including photocopying and recording, or in any information storage or retrieval system without permission in writing from the publishers.

Contents

Acknowledgements	ix
List of Illustrations	x
Preface	xi
Gerald Dawe	

1 | **Introduction** Guy Woodward	1
2 | **The Modernity of Thomas Kilroy** Nicholas Grene	7
3 | **Thomas Kilroy – Irish Modernist: a response to Nicholas Grene** Anthony Roche	21
4 | **The Intellectual on Stage** Thomas Kilroy	29
5 | **Publishing Plays and the Plays of Thomas Kilroy** Peter Fallon	41
6 | **An Extract from the Play 'Blake'** Thomas Kilroy	49
7 | **Panel Discussion 1: Reading Kilroy**	59
8 | **Panel Discussion 2: Directing Kilroy**	75
9 | **Thomas Kilroy in Conversation with Adrian Frazier**	89
Poem: 'Tom Kilroy's Big Country' Gerard Fanning	101
Notes on contributors	103
Index	109

Acknowledgements

The co-ordinating committee for 'Across the Boundaries: Talking about Thomas Kilroy' was comprised of Gerald Dawe (chair), Lilian Foley, Jason McElligott, and Caoimhe Ní Lochlainn (TCD); Jessica Traynor and Aideen Howard (the Abbey Theatre); Stephen Wilmer and Francis Thackaberry (the Samuel Beckett Centre, TCD).

The symposium was made possible through the financial support of the School of English and the Trinity Long Room Hub, Trinity College Dublin. The staging of 'Blake' was made possible by a grant from UNESCO City of Literature to whom kind acknowledgement is made.

In Trinity we wish to thank Julie Bates, Jane Deasy, Donnacha Dennehy, Maura Horan, Orla McCarthy, Simon Williams, and former Provost John Hegarty, whilst the support of the Arts and Social Benefaction Fund, the Samuel Beckett Theatre and the Trinity Foundation were also vital to the success of the symposium.

We also thank Mairead Delaney and the Abbey Theatre Literary Office, *The Irish Times*, Kevin Reynolds and the RTÉ Radio Drama Department, Jane Alger of Unesco City of Literature, Chris Agee and *Irish Pages*, Kieran Hoare and the Archives Collections at the James Hardiman Library, NUI Galway, George C. Heslin, Gerard Smyth, and Carmel Naughton.

Finally we thank Thomas Kilroy for his help during the organization of the symposium and particularly for all his assistance and advice with the preparation of this volume.

List of Illustrations

Frontispiece: Thomas Kilroy with his dog Mitzi at his home in Kilmaine, County Mayo (By kind permission of Robert Hanvey).

1 Cover and centre pages of programme for *The Death and Resurrection of Mr. Roche*, Abbey Theatre, Dublin, 1973 (By kind permission of the Abbey Theatre).
2 Tom (Jordan) Murphy, Clive Geraghty and Ray McBride in *The Death and Resurrection of Mr. Roche*, Abbey Theatre, 1989. Photo: Amelia Stein (By kind permission of the Abbey Theatre).
3 Stephen Brennan, John Molloy, Clive Geraghty, Ingrid Craigie (kneeling) and Eileen Colgan in *Talbot's Box*, Peacock Theatre, Dublin, 1977. Photo: Fergus Bourke (By kind permission of the Abbey Theatre).
4 Poster for *The Death and Resurrection of Mr. Roche*, Olympia Theatre, Dublin, 1968 (By kind permission of the Olympia Theatre and the Dublin Theatre Festival).
5 Jane Brennan, Kevin Murphy and Robert O'Mahoney in *The Secret Fall of Constance Wilde*, Abbey Theatre, 1997. Photo: Amelia Stein (By kind permission of the Abbey Theatre).
6 Cover of programme for *Tea and Sex and Shakespeare*, Rough Magic Theatre Company, 1988. (By kind permission of the Rough Magic Theatre Company)
7 Thomas Kilroy, notes for *Talbot's Box* (Thomas Kilroy Collection, James Hardiman Library, NUI Galway, P103/91 (27)) (By kind permission of Thomas Kilroy and the James Hardiman Library).
8 Aoife Duffin in *Christ Deliver Us!*, Abbey Theatre, 2010. Photo: Ros Kavanagh (By kind permission of Ros Kavanagh).
9 Thomas Kilroy, notes for *Tea and Sex and Shakespeare* (Thomas Kilroy Collection, P103/76 (1)).
10 Thomas Kilroy, typescript and revisions to *Tea and Sex and Shakespeare* (Thomas Kilroy Collection, P103/79 (1)).
11 Cover of programme for *The Death and Resurrection of Mr. Roche*, Hampstead Theatre Club, London, 1969. (By kind permission of the Hampstead Theatre).

Preface

Gerald Dawe

A little over forty years ago Thomas Kilroy's Booker-nominated novel *The Big Chapel* (1971) was published, following on from the success of his play, *The Death and Resurrection of Mr. Roche* (1968). In the years that followed Kilroy has produced an extraordinary body of work for the theatre, and has made a unique contribution to Irish literary and cultural life – a contribution that has been increasingly recognized in recent years with several significant awards, including the Irish PEN/A.T. Cross Award for Literature, *The Irish Times*/ESB Lifetime Achievement Award, the establishment of the Thomas Kilroy Collection at the National University of Ireland, Galway and his election to an Honorary Fellowship at Trinity College Dublin in April 2011.

That same month, the symposium 'Across the Boundaries: Talking about Thomas Kilroy' offered a timely opportunity to pause and gather together an informed group of theatre practitioners, writers and academics to consider the work of one of Ireland's leading playwrights. Nicholas Grene's keynote lecture and Anthony Roche's enthusiastic response set the tone for what turned out to be an inspiring and vivifying weekend of talks and discussions by an extraordinary range of participants from many countries, who addressed Kilroy as both theatre practitioner and writer. This culminated in the staged reading of his play 'Blake' with a remarkable group of Abbey actors under the direction of Patrick Mason in the Samuel Beckett Theatre, and was rounded off with the generous re-broadcasting by RTÉ of the specially commissioned radio play *In the Garden of the Asylum*. All in all, 'Across the Boundaries' was an emphatic reminder of just how prolific and profound Kilroy's achievement has been in both Irish and international terms.

The programme of events at Trinity, kindly hosted by the Trinity Long Room Hub in association with the Oscar Wilde Centre, the School of English, the Samuel Beckett Centre, the Abbey Theatre, and the RTÉ Radio Drama Department was funded in part by Dublin UNESCO City of Literature.

I would like to offer our thanks, first and foremost, to Jason McElligott, a tireless advocate of research and learning at Trinity Long Room Hub, and now Keeper at Marsh's Library, Dublin. Dr McElligott was a wonderful colleague during the planning of 'Across the Boundaries' while doing a million other equally pressing things.

In helping to organize the event Lilian Foley, administrator of the Oscar Wilde Centre, was as ever an example of diligence and care; Francis Thackaberry at the Samuel Beckett Centre, Caoimhe Ní Lochlainn of Trinity's Communication Office, Aideen Howard and Jessica Traynor at the Abbey Theatre, Kevin Reynolds of RTÉ and Jane Alger of UNESCO City of Literature all helped to make the whole thing work. Each and every one made the boundaries crossable with ease and good spirit.

Under the guidance of the then Provost John Hegarty, Trinity College has become involved in fostering and developing new collaborative partnerships – college-wide, country-wide and internationally – of creative arts, technologies and culture. 'Across the Boundaries' is one of the earliest expressions of that initiative, from which we can see what is possible when resources are pooled and focused.

With this impressive publication of *Across the Boundaries: Talking about Thomas Kilroy*, deftly edited by Guy Woodward, the work of that creative weekend in the Trinity Long Room Hub, together with other important new material, should find a wider audience and marks a further step in the recognition of Thomas Kilroy as one of Ireland's finest artists.

1 | Introduction

Guy Woodward

> What I want, more than anything, is a theatre which can hold – danger. Where danger can detonate upon a stage. You see, I believe if theatre can do that, there will be less – danger left in the world. Our only hope is that art transforms the human animal. Nothing else has worked.
>
> *The Madame MacAdam Travelling Theatre*[1]

'Across the Boundaries: Talking about Thomas Kilroy' was a symposium held in Trinity College Dublin in April 2011, curated by Professor Gerald Dawe, lecturer in the School of English and Director of the Oscar Wilde Centre for Irish Writing. This unique gathering brought together scholars and theatre practitioners from Ireland, Britain and the United States to revisit, discuss and celebrate the work of Thomas Kilroy. This book provides a record of the occasion and gathers together edited versions of the lectures, talks and discussions that took place over the weekend, together with an interview between Kilroy and Adrian Frazier which took place at NUI Galway a month before the symposium in March 2011. We also publish for the first time an extract, selected by the author, from his play 'Blake', a rehearsed reading of which was performed on the final evening of 'Across the Boundaries' in the Samuel Beckett Theatre in Trinity, directed by Patrick Mason with a cast drawn from the Abbey Theatre.

Somewhat remarkably, this symposium was the first such gathering devoted to Thomas Kilroy. Considering the scale of his achievement and

---

[1] Thomas Kilroy, *The Madame MacAdam Travelling Theatre* (London: Methuen Drama, 1991), p. 25.

the measure of respect in which he is held by his creative peers and by theatre critics, critical appraisal of his work remains at a relatively early stage. In 1994 Anthony Roche wrote in the introduction to his study *Contemporary Irish Drama* that, alone of the writers under examination, he had decided to address Kilroy's plays individually because they were 'still (undeservedly) the least known and lacking in critical treatment'.[2] The intervening years have seen the publication of a special edition of the *Irish University Review* dedicated to Kilroy's work (2002) and Thierry Dubost's monograph *The Plays of Thomas Kilroy* (2007), but much work clearly remains to be done, and the attendance and participation of younger generations of scholars at the symposium was hugely encouraging in this respect. It is also pleasing to be able to include in this volume images of a selection of documents from the Thomas Kilroy Collection held at the James Hardiman Library at NUI Galway, a resource which presents rich opportunities for future researchers.

In his essay in this volume on publishing the work of Thomas Kilroy, Peter Fallon describes the writer as a 'bridge-builder', and the symposium had similar and conscious ambitions. Kilroy's work as a playwright, lecturer and literary critic over more than five decades connects the creative and the critical modes of writing with rare imagination and precision, and it is fitting that contributors to 'Across the Boundaries' were drawn from both the academic and theatrical spheres. In his essay 'Groundwork for an Irish Theatre', published in 1959, Kilroy wrote that 'it is useful to look upon the theatre as a community, at its best an exuberant, self-educating community with the individual members influencing one another and the group as a whole very responsive to the demands of society about it'.[3] In revisiting, discussing and celebrating Kilroy's writings, it is hoped that this book presents a portrait of a similarly mutually supportive community, following his own preference for collaboration in the form of 'The Workshop', as he described it in that essay. This has been a guiding principle throughout Kilroy's career, and as he writes in a new essay 'The Intellectual on Stage' in this volume, 'Without the group there is no theatre'.

Kilroy's role as a builder of bridges is abundantly illustrated by many of the contributions to this volume. Although his dramatic art has

---

[2] Anthony Roche, *Contemporary Irish Drama: From Beckett to McGuinness* (Dublin: Gill and Macmillan, 1994), p. 7.
[3] Thomas Kilroy, 'Groundwork for an Irish Theatre', *Studies. An Irish Quarterly Review of Letters, Philosophy and Science*, 48:190 (Summer 1959), 192-8 (p. 192).

insistently and unrepentantly dissented from the naturalistic tradition prevalent in modern Irish theatre, it is notable that directors including Lynne Parker and Michael Scott have chosen to present his plays within naturalistic settings, as they describe in the 'Directing Kilroy' discussion (Scott speaks of his concern for accuracy in the matter of the light switches and cutlery used in his production of *Ghosts*.). In 'Reading Kilroy' Declan Hughes describes how the contrast between the setting and the events unfolding on stage in the revised version of *Tea and Sex and Shakespeare* enables a rarely seen and exciting dialogue between naturalistic and non-naturalistic theatrical modes. Furthermore, the postmodern elements of Kilroy's plays, and his radical adaptations of works by Chekhov, Ibsen, Pirandello and Wedekind, have forged new connections between the Irish and European dramatic spheres, and between nineteenth and twentieth-century dramatic modes and historical narratives. In *Ghosts* Mrs Aylward observes to Father Manning that 'In this country we are so good at concealment': recasting that play in Ireland of the 1980s results in a deeply political and devastating critique of delusional clerical hypocrisies and the power wielded by the Catholic church over communities and the life of the individual alike; similarly, the relocation of Wedekind's *Spring Awakening* as *Christ Deliver Us!* to Ireland of the late 1940s permits a keenly prescient interrogation of the traumatic experiences of children in church schools and institutions.[4]

Kilroy's enduring concern with the Second World War likewise reflects a singular ability to reposition mid-twentieth-century Ireland within European historical narratives. This is amply demonstrated by *Double Cross*, *The Madame MacAdam Travelling Theatre*, *Christ Deliver Us!* and, as he suggests in the interview with Frazier, by ongoing fictional projects. In *Madame MacAdam* a distant bomber is heard in a provincial town south of the border, and Mr Grainger's fulminations in *Christ Deliver Us!* further suggest that the war has comprehensively denied the possibility of further cultural or political isolation:

> I blame the Hitler war, Canon. Nothing will ever be the same again after that war. Mr De Valera may have protected this country and kept the war from our shores. Still! The devil is out! Breakdown. Once upon a time everything was in its place. Not anymore. Look at the filth in the picture-houses! Foreign

---

[4] Thomas Kilroy, *Ghosts* (Oldcastle, Co Meath: Gallery Press, 2002), p. 29.

influences! We may not have been invaded before. But we're being invaded now!⁵

Many of Kilroy's plays are centred upon figures from political and literary history, but this book should enable a greater appreciation of the biographical and historical contexts from which and in which these works themselves have emerged. In the interview with Adrian Frazier, Kilroy describes his childhood in Callan, County Kilkenny, during the Emergency and the conservative and anti-intellectual socio-cultural atmosphere of Dublin in the 1950s and 60s from which his earliest writings arose. One of the great strengths of this collection is its recording of a number of testimonies, from Nicholas Grene and Anthony Roche in particular, to the powerful impact of Kilroy's plays, for those who were unable or were too young to have witnessed some of the original productions.

In conversation with Frazier, Kilroy calls attention to the spatial awareness he brings to bear on each play as it evolves, stating that 'It's in answering technical problems [...] that the form of the play finally emerges'. Another aspect of his writing craft is celebrated by several contributors, however, who note the care with which Thomas Kilroy uses language, and affirm the importance of his plays as written pieces apart from their life on the stage. Peter Fallon is forthright in arguing for the importance of the existence of the plays as printed texts, as a means of ensuring their afterlife in the hands of future readers. Lynne Parker describes Kilroy's work as a 'relief' to read, 'as the work of someone who is not afraid to be articulate and to write eloquent English', and Christopher Murray observes that Kilroy 'is both a literary and a theatrical writer; it's not really feasible to distinguish one language from the other in his case'.

Kilroy's plays are written with a profound understanding of the elements needed for successful staging, but are much more than blueprints for production, and seem crafted with an eye on their reception as written documents: here he has been brilliantly served by Gallery Press. His evident relish for performance and statement, and his restless and invigorating concern for self-definition and redefinition are evident on the page as well as the stage. And indeed, aside from the technical, spatial and visual inventiveness and theatricality of the plays, the sheer Wildean quotability of the plays should also be celebrated: in *Double Cross*, for example, Lord Beaverbrook describes the British Empire as 'the greatest compromise between democracy and élitism

---

⁵ Thomas Kilroy, *Christ Deliver Us!* (Oldcastle, Co. Meath: Gallery Press, 2010), p. 55.

ever devised by human political ingenuity'; in *Ghosts* Oliver Aylward observes that 'There is more evil propagated inside family life than in any other human organization that I know of'; and in *The Secret Fall of Constance Wilde* Oscar himself declares that 'I was born of the union of a small, bearded goat and a walking historical monument. This accounts for the confusion of Dionysian and Apollonian elements in my make-up'.

As Peter Fallon notes, Kilroy's work is rarely performed and has been little revived. I hope that this volume will help to stimulate interest in doing so – contributors to the discussions spoke with enthusiasm about the prospect of future productions of Kilroy's work, and as Christina Hunt Mahony observes, it may be that newer generations of theatregoers are more accustomed to onstage postmodernity. However, Kilroy is appraised here for more than his dramatic art alone. His 1971 novel *The Big Chapel* is re-evaluated and rightly acknowledged as a hugely significant work; some may join me in regretting that Kilroy has not, as yet, published further prose fiction, or indeed regret the fact that no volume of collected literary criticism has appeared to date.

Thomas Kilroy celebrates his eightieth birthday in 2014 and we should cherish his presence. The form of the symposium allowed for more personal reflections than are often permitted by academic discourse, a feature that is deliberately reproduced in this publication. The following talks and discussions convey the enormous warmth and affection for this most astringent and committed of writers, and this volume hopefully goes some way towards repaying his consistent generosity to students, scholars and theatre practitioners alike over many decades.

2 | The Modernity of Thomas Kilroy

Nicholas Grene

In 1972 I read an essay on 'Synge and Modernism' by Thomas Kilroy that he had given as a lecture at the Synge Centenary conference the previous year. I was in the final stages of writing my doctoral dissertation on Synge, in that dreadful state of anxious aggressiveness where I felt obliged to dismiss or quarrel with everyone else who wrote about my man. With Kilroy's essay, however, I could not quarrel, because he placed Synge in a perspective quite unlike that of previous critics. He brought to the subject a new breadth of vision, a critical intelligence and authority which I could only envy and admire. He started by observing how the 'exuberant, determined provincialism' of the early Irish dramatic movement seemed to involve a 'rejection of what is central to European drama of the same period'.[1] He then went on to identify the special position of Synge in this: 'he cannot be simply accommodated within the early Abbey Theatre Movement and left there'. Kilroy maintained that Synge's work could be associated with some of the characteristics of European modernism. He summed up Synge's sensibility as 'private, intensely preoccupied with the nature of human freedom [...] secular but committed to the essential spirituality of human action, subversive of the main, middle culture of which Modernism is the counter-culture'.[2] That still seems to me an astonishingly penetrating analysis of Synge's vision. But it was Kilroy's ability to look at Synge within the broad context of modernism, to take him out of that often retold story of the early Abbey – 'Give up Paris [...] Go to the Aran Islands' and all that – which was to me so very exciting.

---

[1] Thomas Kilroy, 'Synge and Modernism', in Maurice Harmon (ed.), *J.M. Synge Centenary Papers 1971* (Dublin: Dolmen Press, 1972), pp. 167-79.
[2] ibid., p. 170.

Synge in this essay is re-imagined not as the 'last Romantic' but as a forerunner of the modern Irish theatre that Thomas Kilroy has done so much to conceive, energize and create. His 1959 *Studies* essay 'Groundwork for an Irish Theatre' is now generally recognized as a key manifesto for the extraordinary renewal that was to come in the next decade. In that essay, he appeals to models being established in the British theatre of the time, Joan Littlewood's Theatre Workshop that had launched the career of Behan, and the English Stage Company at the Royal Court that had pioneered the work of Osborne and Wesker. He looks to an ethos that will bring the writer back into the theatre. The essay ends with a rhetorical flourish centring on the new Abbey then being re-built: 'Very shortly a building will rise from the rubble in Marlborough Street. Is it fanciful to imagine that in this building there will be found two, three, or five years hence, a group of young Irish dramatists forging in splendid co-operation with their fellow artists the uncreated conscience of their race?'[3] It was to be seven more years before that building was completed, but well before that the young Irish dramatists had begun to appear: Hugh Leonard, Brian Friel, Tom Murphy, Eugene McCabe and of course Thomas Kilroy himself. They were not all immediately welcomed in the Abbey, and the Ernest Blythe era had still some time to run before imaginative directors such as Tomás Mac Anna would be given their heads. But the Irish theatre that Kilroy forecast in 1959, innovative in its dramaturgy and capable of representing adequately the realities of a modernizing Ireland, the 1960s version of the Joycean 'uncreated conscience' of the race, was burgeoning by the end of the decade.

In choosing 'The Modernity of Thomas Kilroy' for my title I had in mind two central features of Kilroy's achievement. He is one of the great modernizers of the Irish theatre, in his critical reflections but most importantly in his own creative practice. He has found all sorts of exciting ways of liberating us from what had become the deadly model of the Abbey play with its recognizable small town setting, its surface realism, its predictable shape and structure. From his first written play *The O'Neill* through the brilliant conception of *Talbot's Box* and *Double Cross* to the radical dramaturgy of *The Secret Fall of Constance Wilde*, he has transformed the nature of theatrical representation within our tradition. At the same time, he has reached out to the major classics of European drama – Chekhov's *Seagull*, Pirandello's *Six Characters*, Wedekind's *Spring Awakening* – and adapted them to an Irish idiom

---

[3] Kilroy, 'Groundwork for an Irish Theatre', *Studies* (Summer 1959), p. 198.

and an Irish situation. This is where his modernizing theatrical practice overlaps with the other dimension of his work which I want to discuss, his critical awareness of the social and political life of modern Ireland. *The Death and Resurrection of Mr. Roche* is obviously a landmark play here, with its evocation of the subterranean repressed male sexuality of its time. But many of Kilroy's plays that are not set in the contemporary period use the prism of history to force audiences to reflect upon their own present. *Talbot's Box* mediates always between the early twentieth century of its protagonist and the 1970s when it was written and staged. Both his Field Day plays, *Double Cross* and *The Madame MacAdam Travelling Theatre*, illuminate the 1980s by their evocation of figures from earlier periods. *Secret Fall* and *Christ Deliver Us!* do not represent directly the horrors of the abuse of children that have so haunted our society in the last twenty years, but in their own way they speak powerfully to that knowledge. I want, therefore, to talk about Kilroy as a modernizer of Irish theatre and a dramatic witness to the emerging modernity of Ireland.

1. Modernism

The O'Neill was not staged until 1969, the year after *The Death and Resurrection of Mr. Roche,* but it seems that it was written first, and was turned down for production very regretfully by Hilton Edwards of the Gate Theatre in 1964 on the grounds that he could not afford to stage such a large scale play. The play is concerned with the figure of Hugh O'Neill, leader of the Irish in the Nine Years War, the last major rebellion against British colonial control at the end of the sixteenth century. His story is a dramatic one, encompassing an English upbringing, his double position as the Earl of Tyrone and as The O'Neill, the Gaelic leader of his clan, his marriage to Mabel Bagenal, sister of one of the English generals he fought against, his success in uniting Ireland against the Crown, followed by the catastrophe of the Battle of Kinsale and his eventual enforced flight from Ireland. It was to provide Brian Friel with the subject for his fine play *Making History*, staged by Field Day in 1988 and was also the subject of an amateur student play in which I had a part in Trinity in 1966. I played The O'Donnell, the other earl of the Flight of the Earls, and as I remember my main function was to die of a fever in Rome in the second act, feverishly declaiming nostalgic memories of my native Donegal. 'Tons of buttermilk' is the only phrase I can recall of my lines. What none of us realized at the time was that Kilroy had already made this clank clunk sort of historical drama obsolete with his way of telling the story.

In *The O'Neill* each of the two acts starts at the same moment, the Battle of the Yellow Ford in 1598, the high point of success for the Irish in the Nine Years War. In both cases the triumph of O'Neill is framed by a conversation between Robert Cecil, Queen Elizabeth's Secretary of State, and Mountjoy, the Lord Deputy who was eventually to defeat O'Neill. In the first act, this involves a recreation of O'Neill's backstory, including his relationship with Mabel and its disastrous ending when she is unable to tolerate life among the O'Neill clan; in the second it takes us on to Kinsale and the surrender of O'Neill to the English at Mellifont. The presence on stage of Cecil and Mountjoy makes us always aware of the ultimate historical outcome, the inevitable final crushing of Irish resistance by the superior forces of the English, but Kilroy uses a fluid and flexible dramaturgy to render the complex figure of O'Neill and the conflicting factors in the historical situation that confronts him. It is no simple nationalist drama of Ireland versus England. To start with, there is the constant warring between and within the Irish clans. There is a grisly recollection by Mabel of fellow clansmen hacking Phelim Mac Turlach O'Neill to death and drowning his young son, while she and O'Neill stood by and watched. There is the English Master Mountfort, who sees the Irish rebellion only in terms of the pan-European Catholic cause of the Counter-Reformation. O'Neill throughout is the reluctant hero, initially resistant to the passionate love of Mabel, resistant to the more hot-headed of his own followers, doubtful of the vision of Mountfort, always disposed to temporize in the interest of a longer term game that no-one will allow him to play his way.

What is distinctive about the play is the fact that at no point is the audience meant to be under the illusion that these events of the past are being played out in reality on stage. When Cecil and Mountjoy in the opening scene decide they need to go over O'Neill's past, O'Neill himself is made part of that rehearsal. At a gesture from O'Neill, his followers 'disassemble the set' of the Yellow Ford battlefield and leave the stage empty.[4] Much of the action from then on is seen from the viewpoint of three Irish spies, Thadie Mahon, Patrick M'Art Moyle and Gillaboy O'Flannigan. They speak in a clownishly colloquial style set off against the more standard prose in which most of the dialogue is written. They are recurrently present to provide a sharply satiric distancing device, counterpointing the high seriousness of the history play. It is possible that they might have been suggested by the four knights in Eliot's

---

[4] Thomas Kilroy, *The O'Neill* (Oldcastle, Co. Meath: Gallery Press, 1995), p. 13.

Murder in the Cathedral, who after their killing of Thomas à Becket disconcertingly step out of their historical roles to address the audience directly. But where Eliot confines himself to this one metatheatrical shock tactic, it is part of Kilroy's strategy throughout the play to break down the illusionist principle of theatrical representation. *The O'Neill* brings Irish historical drama up to date with an improvisatory, quick-change, non-linear narrative in place of the standard beginning and middle to end dramatic structure.

Kilroy rarely uses the naturalist convention of the fourth wall, the pretence that an audience is looking in at a realistic room from which the fourth wall has been removed. But one of the most radical challenges to that convention in his work came with *Talbot's Box*, directed by Patrick Mason at the Peacock in 1977. At the start of the play, 'the lights reveal a huge box occupying virtually the whole stage, its front closed to the audience. The effect should be that of a primitive, enclosed space, part prison, part sanctuary, part acting space'.5 There is no pretence that the box is other than an acting space; when it is opened outwards, all the actors, costumes and props are already in place. We begin with the corpse of Matt Talbot in the morgue in 1925, but the four actors that surround him play a variety of parts, including a Priest Figure (taken by a woman actor) giving a pious sermon on the extraordinary devotion of Talbot, the reformed drunkard who lived so many years with chains beneath his clothes as a penance of mortification. The tone is satiric and parodic. But then there is an extraordinary moment, as the dead body

> rises on the trolley and flings both arms out in the shape of crucifixion. As he does so, blinding beams of light shoot through the walls of the box, pooling about him and leaving the rest of the stage in darkness. The other four figures shrink away, the women screaming. A high-pitched wailing cry rises, scarcely human but representing human beings in great agony. As it reaches its crescendo it is of physical discomfort to the audience. The four figures race about, hands aloft, to block the lights.6

The theatre as a box, an empty space, is not only a place of make-believe but a place of revelation.

To some extent, it seems to me, *Talbot's Box* can be related to German expressionism, the forms used by Kaiser and Toller in the 1920s where a phantasmagoric journey of the protagonist allows for an

---

[5] Thomas Kilroy, *Talbot's Box* (Dublin: Gallery Press, 1979), p. 11.
[6] ibid., p. 19.

investigation of the society around him. It is the model used by Denis Johnston in *The Old Lady Says 'No!'* (1929). In the case of Talbot, the society evoked is that of his own time, when he was reviled as a scab for working through the 1913 Dublin lockout, and the 1970s, when the movement for his canonization was at its height: in 1975 Pope Paul VI declared him Venerable Matt Talbot. Within this structure Kilroy manages also to talk back to earlier Irish drama. For instance, at the beginning of the second act of the play, there is the O'Caseyan figure resembling Captain Boyle, whom we hear screaming with irritation at Talbot's hymn-singing. This transmutes into Talbot's memories of his own alcoholic wife-beating father, simultaneously providing a reproof of O'Casey's comic version of the bad marriage and a way into the psychological conditioning of Talbot's childhood. The distinctive achievement of the play, however, is its refusal to offer a reductive view of Talbot as a mere psychopathological phenomenon. The genuine strangeness of his vision is treated with imaginative respect, all the more so because of Talbot's inability ever fully to communicate it. For him God is a darkness within, unrelated to the charade-like forms of worship of the church. The paradox that the play brings out is the fundamental aloneness of the mystic who is taken by the Christian community as exemplary, but who can only achieve that state by a denial of communal attachment and connection.

Kilroy uses all the available resources of the theatre inventively and imaginatively. Take the case of mediated images in *Double Cross*. The striking design of the play is to match the stories of Brendan Bracken, British superpatriot, Churchill's Minister for Information during the Second World War, and William Joyce, supertraitor, the infamous Lord Haw Haw of German propaganda broadcasts. Both were Irishmen with simulated identities, overcompensating (as Kilroy sees it) for the traumas of their Irish childhoods. The drama is divided into a 'Bracken play' set in London and a 'Joyce play' set in Berlin. But in both parts the conflict between the two is sharpened by the presence on video screen of the absent antagonist, jeering and insulting. By this point in the twenty-first century the use of video projections has become practically a required part of any live theatre production, often a fussily obtrusive and unnecessary intrusion. In the case of *Double Cross* they work as part of the fundamental fabric of the play, which is all about constructed images. And the virtual presences on screen and radio broadcast only help to accentuate the virtuoso performance on stage of both Bracken and Joyce by the same actor. No-one who saw Stephen Rea metamorphose from Bracken to Joyce without leaving the stage will ever forget it. The sheer skill of the living actor who can so transform himself before us, counterpointed with recorded versions of face and voice, made for a supremely theatrical way of dramatizing the constructed nature of human personality.

There is no one template for a Kilroy play; he uses the techniques, the forms and the playing styles that fit the subject in hand. So for *The Secret Fall of Constance Wilde* it was puppets and puppetry that provided the idiom for a play about assumed roles both voluntary and involuntary. The Japanese tradition of bunraku seems to have been the initial inspiration, bunraku in which onstage puppetmaster manipulators are deemed invisible because clothed all in black. Kilroy's puppeteers or 'attendant figures' are very different, however. This is how the play opens: 'A dark stage. The attendant figures, mute, emerge out of the darkness: white, faceless masks, bowler hats, chequered pants, white gloves, a cross between Victorian toffs and street theatre performers, stage-hands and puppeteers, dressers, waiters and Figures of Fate'.[7] They roll out on to the stage a 'great white disk', which becomes the acting space on which Constance, Oscar and Alfred Douglas play out their tortured drama. It is a memory play in so far as the action begins after Wilde's imprisonment and release, as he pleads to be allowed to see his children and rages against Constance's refusal to allow him to do so. From there, it moves back through the history of the Wildes' marriage, their first meeting in Merrion Square, Oscar's love affair with Douglas, and all the terrible consequences of that relationship. In some sense, it resembles Yeats's concept of 'dreaming back', the compulsive re-living by the dead of the traumatic events of their lives: both Constance and Oscar are in fact close to death. But the onstage puppeteers embody an added sense of the performative nature of the roles the three principals play. They are locked into the parts of their shared emotional drama; at the same time the Victorian-costumed manipulators emphasize how far those parts are shaped and conditioned by the society in which they live.

Wilde subtitled *Lady Windermere's Fan*, his first society comedy, 'A Play About A Good Woman', hinting at the play's denouement in which Mrs Erlynne, the scandalous blackmailing vamp, rather than her high-principled puritanical daughter, is revealed as the 'good woman'. Kilroy's strategy is to reverse that process. Oscar in frustrated anger in the first scene rails against his wife's morality: 'Constance, you

---

[7] Thomas Kilroy, *The Secret Fall of Constance Wilde* (Oldcastle, Co. Meath: Gallery Press, 1997), p. 11.

positively drip with goodness'.[8] Constance, however, is resistant to this image of herself: 'Never again will I be invented as the good woman'.[9] The play makes Constance Wilde the dramatic centre of attention, where in the standard version of her story she is merely the good and loyal wife betrayed by her histrionic husband and his irresponsible lover. That stereotype, we are made to feel, is simply a way of denying to her any inner life of her own. As Kilroy re-imagines the marriage of the Wildes, they are brought together initially by the reactions of both against their fathers, what Oscar refers to as 'a mutual interest in patricide'.[10] The psychological consequences of the bad father are pursued in Kilroy's companion play *My Scandalous Life*, dramatizing Alfred Douglas in later life. What is never fully revealed until the end of *Secret Fall* is Constance's sexual abuse by her father, the 'secret fall' that has made her feel contaminated with evil, anything but the 'good woman' she is called.

What gives this play its extraordinary impact is the way in which the inner psychological dramas of the three central figures are played out in theatrically embodied images. The Wilde children are represented by miniature manikins worked by the attendants. There is a heartbreaking moment when they scamper away from Constance on the beach, and she, painfully crippled from her – literal – fall on the staircase, cannot run after them. The shape-changing nature of beauty to which Wilde is attracted is revealed in the various metamorphoses of Douglas, appearing as a Christ-like priest figure to Wilde in prison before finally standing naked as the ideal of the Androgyne. Puppetry makes visible a mental landscape in which the miniaturized children are counterpointed with a figure more than life size. Gordon Craig wanted to reduce the live actor to an Űber-marionette, but Kilroy instead figures the horror of the father's sexual abuse acted out in Constance's memory as a 'gigantic puppet: Victorian gentleman, red cheeks, black moustache, bowler hat, umbrella, frock coat'.[11] *The Secret Fall of Constance Wilde* is a dazzling display of what theatre is and can do, at once beautiful ritual performance, searing human drama and the deepest projections of the psyche.

Kilroy is a modernist playwright who has assimilated the dramaturgy of his great European predecessors, Ibsen, Strindberg, Chekhov, Pirandello, Brecht. As one of the epigraphs to his 1977 essay

---

[8] ibid., p. 12.
[9] ibid., p. 13.
[10] ibid., p. 23.
[11] ibid., p. 66.

on Yeats and Beckett he uses a quotation from Artaud, mad prophet of the theatrical avant-garde: 'I say that the stage is a concrete physical place which asks to be filled, and to be given its own concrete language to speak'.[12] That essay remains one of the most piercingly intelligent analyses of Yeats and Beckett. The two playwrights are placed within a 'modern dramatic tradition [...] that subscribes to the integrity, the wholeness, the autonomy of stage-practice, one which undermines the idea of humanist imitation which has long dominated the European theatre'.[13] Yeats and Beckett are seen as exemplary in their privileging of a theatrical idiom of image and movement, Artaud's 'concrete language', over a representational drama of speech. In the works of both dramatists, as Kilroy sees it, the stage is an autonomous domain, not dependent on its evocation of any extra-theatrical reality. The two stand out, implicitly, against the traditional view of Irish drama as dominated by language, the 'sovereignty of words', and Kilroy is evidently with them on this. His too is a self-reflexive theatre, not one of illusionist representation or realistic dialogue. But there is a major difference between Kilroy's practice and that of Yeats or Beckett. He is specifically concerned with the social and political realities of the Ireland in which he writes, and these are the direct or indirect subject of many of his plays. This takes me on to the matter of Kilroy's rendering of Irish modernity.

2. Modernity

How do we define the modern, and where does it start? The re-titling of what we used to call the Renaissance period as 'early modern' pushes the start date back to the sixteenth century; others would see the nineteenth century as the crucial period. R.F. Foster's influential history *Modern Ireland* (1988) runs from 1600 to 1972, while Joseph Lee's *The Modernisation of Irish Society* (1973) covers the period 1848 to 1918. However historians may see modernity in the broadest terms as changes in the organization of the state or economic practices, one crucial shift in Ireland came midway through the twentieth century when a predominantly rural and agricultural country started to become increasingly urbanized. The publication of T.K. Whitaker's government white paper on *Economic Development* in 1958 is often taken as the point at which the inward-looking, protectionist Ireland of de Valera

---

[12] Cited in Thomas Kilroy, 'Two Playwrights: Yeats and Beckett', in Joseph Ronsley (ed.), *Myth and Reality in Irish Literature* (Waterloo, Ont.: Wilfrid Laurier University Press, 1977), pp. 183-95 (p. 183).
[13] ibid., p. 184.

was brought to an end. Certainly, looking back to the small village in Co Wicklow where I grew up in the 1950s, it seems more than a lifetime away from the commuter-belt appendage of Dublin it has all but become now. One part of Kilroy's achievement has been to dramatize that time of transitional modernization during the 1950s and 1960s. Beyond that, however, he has returned repeatedly to earlier periods to stage the repressions that have returned upon us in our own time.

The key play here is *The Death and Resurrection of Mr. Roche*, first staged at the Dublin Theatre Festival in 1968. This is often seen as a breakthrough work, because it was the first play with an overtly gay central character on the Irish stage, but there is much more to it than that. It is an extraordinary evocation of a particular moment in Irish cultural history. As always in Kilroy, the stage setting is important: 'KELLY's basement flat in a Dublin Georgian house and the street outside. The main acting area is the flat itself, well downstage. It is approached first by a fine Georgian door in outline against the backdrop of night or street'.[14] This is a postcolonial Ireland of underground Dublin men: celibate, homo-social, misogynist. There is the owner of the flat, Kelly, a low level civil servant with repressed gay tendencies, as it finally emerges, and Seamus his married schoolteacher friend; along with them we find Myles, the would-be car salesman, and the character known only as the Medical Student, who in fact never passed his exams and works as a morgue attendant. Joining the late night Saturday party after the pubs close are the homosexual Mr Roche and his young friend Kevin, extremely unwelcome guests from Kelly's point of view.

Kelly and Seamus are representative of a whole generation, sons of farmers, small shopkeepers and Guards from down the country, the first in their family to make it to the city and white-collar employment. In their late night cups they remember their country childhoods with a mixture of nostalgia and intense relief at having escaped. Kelly sentimentally imagines an alternative life back home:

> You know, there's something in that – about working on the land, I mean. It's what I'd prefer if I was given the free choice. But the only people who can get land in this country are the bloody Germans. I'd like land. You know, Seamus, you know when you pull a turnip from a wet drill what it's like, with the roots black and wet, lovely to the touch, like silk. That's the land, like food itself. You can't transplant that in concrete, ha?

---

[14] Thomas Kilroy, *The Death and Resurrection of Mr. Roche* (Oldcastle, Co. Meath: Gallery Press, 2002), p. 11.

Seamus, however, is there to counter with the reality: 'Oh, indeed if you were given a parcel of it in the morning you wouldn't take it. It's like everything else – nice at a distance'.[15] These are men who have made the transition from rural to urban, but like the rest of those in the drinking group have failed to get themselves a life. The books that litter Kelly's flat are no longer read; Seamus's marriage, it eventually appears, he feels to be a miserable trap. In the background to the Saturday night debauch is the standard conservative Ireland. Myles lives with his mother; on Sunday morning all of them are off to Mass in a church of the Carmelites, significantly an enclosed order 'beside the Royal Hospital for the Incurables'.[16]

The action of the play takes the form of a carnival celebration that turns into nightmare. The superficial high spirits of the group are expressed in Kelly's songs and recitations of popular American ballads, but aggression builds against Mr Roche as the scapegoat for all their resentments and frustrations. In spite of his known claustrophobia, Roche is bundled down into the 'holy-hole', the tiny cellar in Kelly's flat, where he appears to die. The underground space even deeper within the subterranean home is where active sexual energy must be buried. Yet as the title of the play indicates, Roche is dead but won't stay down. Mr Roche's 'resurrection' is played in a style deliberately marked off from the near naturalism of the rest of the action. When he tells of watching the sunrise, 'the tone', the stage direction tells us, 'should shift radically from all that has gone before', and Mr Roche speaks 'rising ecstatically, priest-like, with arms outstretched, very slowly with menace': 'And-it-came! Like the beginning of life again. A great white egg at the foot of the sky. Breaking up into light. Breaking up into life'.[17] In a letter to Christopher Murray, Kilroy confessed that in the play 'I did have a certain private academic fun in trying to write an ironic version of the old resurrection-fertility comedy'.[18] A part of the irony is that the fertility god here takes the form of a non-reproductive homosexual male. This is the repressed sexuality that is bound to return in Ireland's ignorant and frustrated, culturally starved society. Among the books that Kelly no longer reads are Nietzsche, Rilke and – appropriately enough – Dostoevsky's *Notes from Underground*, from which he in fact quotes: 'I am a sick man. I am a spiteful man. I am an unattractive

---

[15] ibid., p. 58.
[16] ibid., p. 81.
[17] ibid., p. 74.
[18] Christopher Murray, 'The Artist and the Critic', *Irish University Review*, 32.1 (Spring-Summer 2002), 83-94 (p. 87).

man'.[19] Ireland has still a long way to go before it can reach the liberating defiance of a Nietzsche, the transcendentalism of a Rilke, or even the theorized metaphysical underground life of a Dostoevsky.

Modernity came late to Ireland. We did not have the industrial revolution that catapulted other countries into the modernized world of capitalism. Colonial rule and a conservative Catholic Church both made for social retardation. A key feature of Irish modernity has been the felt need to understand our past history, to work out how we came to be where we are now. To this effort Kilroy's plays have made an important contribution. If you take the long view of modernity, then *The O'Neill* can be seen in this light, a dramatization, without illusions, of the end of pre-modern Gaelic Ireland and the forces that brought about this end. His Second World War plays, *Double Cross* and *The Madame MacAdam Travelling Theatre*, both help to reveal the political and psychological deformations of the past. With *Madame MacAdam* we are confronted with the fascistic tendencies just below the surface of Emergency Ireland. In the case of *Double Cross* what haunts Brendan Bracken, the self-created British imperialist, is the memory of a rabidly republican father who despised him as a 'Mammy's pet'. Inadequate sons haunted by nightmarishly threatening fathers are familiar enough across a range of fiction and drama but take on a special significance within the mental landscape of long colonized Ireland, the spectre of authority elsewhere against which there can never be a wholly successful revolt.

Perhaps Kilroy's most powerful indictment to date of the Ireland that preceded our own time is *Christ Deliver Us!*, staged at the Abbey in 2010. It is of course an adaptation of Frank Wedekind's *Spring Awakening*, written originally in the 1890s. And it is a measure of Ireland's cultural belatedness that a play which reflected the repressive atmosphere of fin-de-siècle Germany should transfer so convincingly to an Irish setting in the late 1940s or early 1950s. Wedekind's ironically entitled *Spring Awakening* is a study of the horrors and dangers of adolescent sexuality. Kilroy follows the original quite closely in the main lines of the plot: the contrast between the freethinking Michael and the anxious Mossy, which ends in Mossy's suicide and Michael's incarceration in an industrial school for having tried to enlighten his friend about sex; the tragic death of the fifteen-year-old Winnie whom Michael has made pregnant; the dynamics of the male and female

---

[19] Kilroy, *Death and Resurrection*, p. 25.

groups of schoolchildren, including the discovery by two of the boys of their gay sexuality. The specifics, however, are made convincingly Irish.

We first see the boys in the Diocesan School superintended by its authoritarian cane wielding priests. We are made aware of the class differences of the likes of Michael, from a well-to-do middle-class home, and Mossy, well down the social scale, whose father is in the army. When the scandal breaks after Mossy's suicide, with Michael's attempts at sex education traced back to him, his father insists that Michael be sent to St Joseph's Industrial School run by the Christian Brothers as a 'good, sharp shock to the system'.[20] Michael's father is sufficiently influential to overawe the relatively humane Canon, principal of the Diocesan School, with threats of political intervention. Inside the Industrial School, the stage direction makes clear, the 'boys are different from the college boys, shaven and bruised heads, black eyes, one or two with dirty bandages'.[21] This is the brutalized bottom of the heap of Irish society, a place of physical abuse and futile attempted brainwashing, of vicious catch-as-catch-can aggression among the inmates. The death of Winnie in Kilroy's play also recalls all too uncomfortably Ireland's unreconstructed past. Where in Wedekind the equivalent girl is killed by a botched abortion, Winnie dies alone in an unassisted childbirth which, for those of my generation or older, is a terrible reminder of Anne Lovett of Granard, the fifteen-year-old who came to an exactly similar end in 1984.

Christ Deliver Us! is a frightening dramatization of a terrible time in Ireland, a time of sexual ignorance and repression, of authoritarian exploitation and abuse. That did not stop it from being theatrically exhilarating in Wayne Jordan's fine Abbey production, with the energy of the opening choreographed hurling scene, the beauty of the dance and embrace of the two gay boys later on. The play also has something like an upbeat ending. The final scene of *Spring Awakening* poses real problems for a contemporary adaptation. Wedekind shows Melchior – equivalent to Kilroy's Michael – escaped from the reformatory, finding himself in a cemetery where his lover is buried, inveigled by his dead friend to join him in death. From this he is rescued by a mysterious Masked Man who lures him back towards life. For the Masked Man Kilroy substitutes Fr Seamus, the one fully enlightened priest from the Diocesan School, the only teacher sufficiently cultured to recognize the pictures of naked men and women Michael has given Mossy as reproductions of the old master paintings of Cranach. In the earlier

---

[20] Kilroy, *Christ Deliver Us!*, p. 53.
[21] ibid., p. 51.

school scene, Fr Seamus, asphyxiating from lack of air, has suffered from a severe speech impediment. In the cemetery, apparently laicized, he no longer stutters and his message to Michael is clear:

> Listen to what the temple of your body is saying to you in secret. Attend to its whispers of hope and desire, streaming through your flesh and blood. [...] Be true to your own nature. That's all there is, finding one's manhood, finding one's womanhood, and being true to it, no matter what form it takes. That's what salvation is...[22]

This is the voice of modern Ireland that enables Michael to walk away from the ghosts of Mossy and Winnie.

Thomas Kilroy is a modernist playwright who shows human behaviour as constructed and performative. We play the roles that we have been taught to play, creatures of our parents, our society, our cultural and class milieu. The theatre, however, does not merely reproduce this sort of socially induced role play; it is its own place with its own forms of action and meaning. In Kilroy we are never allowed to forget that we are sharing in that special experience. His drama is anti-illusionist and metatheatrical. We are not witnessing sixteenth-century Irish history enacted in *The O'Neill*, we are watching a contemporary play upon themes from that history. *Talbot's Box* is the stage space itself as well as the mind of Matt Talbot and the communal memory of him; *The Secret Fall of Constance Wilde* takes place in public superintended and directed by theatrical puppeteers. Kilroy's theatre is secular and materialist in so far as it seeks to analyse and demystify human action. And the modern Ireland which his plays so powerfully evoke has stood in much need of such demystification. Yet Kilroy is never a reductive rationalist, never prepared to deny the existence of mystery beyond demystification – hence his sympathetic treatment of a figure such as Talbot or the visionary Blake. I quoted at the beginning his definition of the sensibility of Synge: 'private, intensely preoccupied with the nature of human freedom [...] secular but committed to the essential spirituality of human action'. It is a fine interpretation of Synge but might also stand as an illuminating insight into the extraordinary drama of Thomas Kilroy.

---

[22] ibid., p. 65.

3 | Thomas Kilroy – Irish Modernist: a response to Nicholas Grene

Anthony Roche

It is a pleasure to respond to Nicholas Grene's rich critical exploration of the plays of Thomas Kilroy, a body of work for which I have an unstinting admiration.[1] Like Nicky, I too missed the first production of *Talbot's Box* at the Peacock in 1977. I was in the United States and was still (just) there when Field Day produced *Double Cross* in 1986. But I had been extremely fortunate that my theatre-going as a teenager in the late 1960s coincided with the emergence of Thomas Kilroy as a major force on the Irish stage.

My parents and I attended the premiere of *The Death and Resurrection of Mr. Roche* at the Olympia during the 1968 Dublin Theatre Festival, probably drawn in part by the curiosity of seeing our surname in the title. It featured, as Nicky has mentioned, the first overtly gay character on an Irish stage, the eponymous Mr Roche. Further, Mr Roche was described in the text as 'the queen of Dunleary',[2] where we had always lived. During the interval at the bar, a friend of the family approached my father and said to him: 'You kept it well hid, boy, wha'?' I offer the story to indicate how ready the Irish audience was to confront this new and daring subject matter. I have no doubt that the play was better served in this respect by being premiered as part of the Dublin Theatre Festival, where Irish plays were placed within the European and globalizing context of visiting productions and critics,

---

[1] For Anthony Roche's analysis of Thomas Kilroy's plays, see the chapter 'Kilroy's Doubles' in Anthony Roche, *Contemporary Irish Drama: Second Edition* (Houndmills: Palgrave Macmillan, 2009), pp. 130-57.
[2] Kilroy, *Death and Resurrection*, p. 15.

than had it been put on first at the Abbey, where it had been submitted and rejected.³

Whetted by this encounter with an exciting new playwright, and given my own burgeoning interest in theatre, I made sure to seek out Kilroy's *The O'Neill* when it was staged at the Peacock the following year. I would probably otherwise have avoided it, because it sounded like a product of the genre that flourished at the time, the deadly dramatization of periods of Irish history, often in the open air with the wind half-drowning out the pseudo-Shakespearean lines the actors were shouting as they strode around in Celtic panto costumes (this is my gloss on Nicky's characterization of 'clank clunk' history drama). I'm not sure the Peacock production entirely avoided all these problems, but what registered even then was the centrality and the modernity of the relationship between Hugh O'Neill and Mabel Bagenal. It did so not only because of its sexual frankness; though it had that. All of Kilroy's plays would reveal a bracing awareness of the key role played by sexuality in the construction of identity, and in this way have proved a refreshing alternative to most Irish theatre, which is verbally frank but sexually prudish. The modernizing relationship between Hugh and Mabel is best understood in the light of Brian Friel's *Making History* (1988). In Friel's play, when Archbishop Lombard insists on the marriage being virtually erased from the narrative history he is writing of the O'Neill, Hugh insists on its centrality to his public as well as his private history. Both Kilroy's and Friel's plays provide a deliberate counter strategy to the ineluctable historic tendency of Irish nationalism to write women out of the nationalist narrative: they write them back in and make them central to the power dynamics of the drama. Part of the deliberate transgressiveness of Kilroy's version is the inter-marriage between a Catholic and a Protestant, still a concern in the late 1960s when Catholics were urged not to enter Trinity College by the hierarchy.

Back in Ireland for a few months in 1976, I had the opportunity to see Kilroy's next play, *Tea and Sex and Shakespeare*, at the Abbey, directed by Max Stafford-Clark of the Royal Court (who had been a student at Trinity in the 1960s) and starring the great Donal McCann as the writer Brien. It was exhilarating to see the main stage of the

---

³ See Thomas Kilroy, 'A Playwright's Festival' (pp. 11-19) and Shaun Richards, 'Subjects of "the machinery of citizenship": *The Death and Resurrection of Mr. Roche* and *The Gentle Island*' (pp. 61-74), in *Interactions: Dublin Theatre Festival 1957-2007*, ed. by Nicholas Grene and Patrick Lonergan with Lilian Chambers (Dublin: Carysfort Press, 2008).

national theatre subject to the zany, surrealistic theatrics of Kilroy's play. It also provided a rare instance of the figure of the writer being represented directly, performing the act of cultural production that is writing, rather than being naturalized under the more usual guise/disguise of tramp or teacher. Brian Friel waited until 1997 to place a writer centre stage in *Give Me Your Answer, Do!*, but Friel's writer is a novelist where Kilroy's is unabashedly a playwright. This allows for a hitherto unprecedented degree of meta-theatricality. When at the height of the play's action Brien is asked by his next-door neighbour how he is getting on with his play he replies: 'I'm writing my play all the time, Sylvester. I'm writing my play just now, Sylvester, as I talk to you. Good morning! You see? Dialogue.'[4]

I was given the opportunity to engage critically for the first time with Thomas Kilroy's theatre in 1982 when Maurice Harmon of UCD invited me to give a paper on the writer at that year's Triennial IASIL Conference. Taking the opportunity to read 1977's *Talbot's Box*, I proposed linking the play with Mr Roche through the idea of the *felix culpa* or fortunate fall; both had a death-and-resurrection motif which I thought served to point up the challenge Kilroy's drama offered to the prevailing norms of Irish naturalism. This led me to describe the huge onstage coffin as Kilroy's box of theatrical tricks, suggesting in turn 'a coffin, a confession box, a witness stand, a wooden bulwark constructed by Talbot the carpenter against the encroaching chaos and Thomas Kilroy's own box of theatrical tricks, the props and stratagems of the playwright's trade openly on display.'[5] What I would like to do at this point, especially in the light of Nicky's comments, is to look at how the play engages with the theatrical career of Sean O'Casey. Matt Talbot was an inner-city working-class Dubliner living in the early twentieth century, so it was inevitable that *Talbot's Box* would resonate with verbal and visual echoes of O'Casey (who wrote two plays about the Dublin Lock Out in which Talbot is involved). If, as Nicky has noted, there is a 'talking back' to the Captain Boyle of O'Casey's Dublin trilogy, there is an even more subtle dialogue with the later stages of O'Casey's career, which were marked by an increasingly explicit degree of theatrical (mainly Expressionist) experimentation, an increasingly tin

---

[4] Thomas Kilroy, *Tea and Sex and Shakespeare* (Oldcastle, Co. Meath: Gallery Press, 1998), p. 30.
[5] Anthony Roche, 'The Fortunate Fall: Two Plays by Thomas Kilroy', in *The Irish Writer and the City*, ed. by Maurice Harmon (Gerrards Cross, Bucks. and Totowa, NJ: Colin Smythe and Barnes and Noble Books, 1984), p. 163. See also Anthony Roche, 'Kilroy's Doubles', *Contemporary Irish Drama: Second Edition*, p. 141.

ear with regard to Dublin speech and a life of exile from Ireland and the Abbey. Nicky mentions Denis Johnston's *The Old Lady Says 'No!'*, but that play was at least staged by the Gate when turned down by the Abbey. O'Casey's *The Silver Tassie* (1929), on the other hand, received only two Abbey productions in the next forty years. I would note also that during the 1970s Thomas Kilroy edited a key critical volume, *Twentieth-Century Interpretations of Sean O'Casey* (1975), to which he contributed a trenchant introduction. In place of a critical essay, he supplies the creative offering of *Talbot's Box*, a play which verbally moves with ease from accurate Dublin idiom to a more overtly poetic style without any of O'Casey's over-writing, and brings O'Casey's modernist experiment out of exile and back on to the stage of the Abbey Theatre.[6]

The debate between the creative and the critical increasingly began to characterize the writings of Thomas Kilroy. Or, rather, a piece of critical writing or an adaptation of a pre-existing dramatic text could metamorphose into an original work for the theatre – Chekhov's *The Seagull* was transplanted to the West of Ireland, and more recently Frank Wedekind's *Spring Awakening* was recast as *Christ Deliver Us!* At the Magill Summer School in Donegal in 2008 Kilroy spoke of how *Double Cross*, his play for the Field Day Theatre Company, began. He was visited by Brian Friel and Stephen Rea, Field Day's co-founders, to discuss a contribution to the company. Kilroy had long been intrigued by the curious relationship he perceived between Brendan Bracken, Winston Churchill's Minister for Information during the Second World War, and William Joyce, who made Nazi broadcasts under the name of Lord Haw Haw. Both native-born Irish, these two men had gone to extraordinary lengths to distance themselves from their origins by theatrically constructing and performing alternative identities. Kilroy had originally intended to write a long essay for the Field Day series of cultural pamphlets. But as he talked with his fellow playwright and this most mercurial and gifted of Irish actors, the idea of *Double Cross* emerged, a play in which the lives of the two men consciously doubled and commented on each other. The two roles would be played by the same actor, in this case Rea. Historically, Bracken and Joyce never actually met; most of the scenes play out in either wartime London or Berlin. But, as Nicky rightly observes, technology – the use of a video screen – made it possible for the two characters simultaneously to occupy the same space. When Joyce is in prison awaiting execution for

---

[6] On Kilroy and O'Casey, see Murray, 'Thomas Kilroy: the Artist and the Critic', *Irish University Review*, 32:1 (2002), pp. 87-90.

treason, Bracken appears on the video 'as if behind bars or a grille of iron' and calmly answers Joyce's question by saying he is there because he is 'searching for his brother'.[7] When Brian Friel divided the one character into a Public and Private Gar in *Philadelphia, Here I Come!* in 1964, two actors were required to play the role. More pertinently, six years earlier, Samuel Beckett had used what was then the advanced technology of the tape recorder to represent simultaneously on-stage a sixty-nine-year-old Krapp confronting his thirty-year-younger self through the medium of recorded sound.

In the past decade or so, official Ireland has begun to take account of the Irish who served as soldiers in two World Wars. But the playwrights, as usual, were in the vanguard. Frank McGuinness and Sebastian Barry have both examined the conflicted loyalties of Irish soldiers from north and south at the Somme. But it was Thomas Kilroy in his two plays for the Field Day Theatre Company, first in *Double Cross* and then in *The Madame MacAdam Travelling Theatre*, who examined Ireland during the Second World War, exploring the complex situation beneath its studied mask of neutrality and the euphemistic term 'the Emergency'. The second play moved from cities central to the theatre of war, London and Berlin, to Ireland. What is so unusual about the setting of *Madame MacAdam* is that it is rural, not urban, and that Kilroy for once adopts the recognizable small town setting of the traditional Abbey play. But what disrupts and blows apart the conventionality of the rural setting is its location close to the border. The play unfolds a few miles into the southern state, allowing us to observe the behaviour of Irish citizens towards the world conflict from which they were largely detached, but close enough to Northern Ireland and the German bombing it suffered for the 'distant sound of a bomber' to be the first sound that is heard.[8] The theatrical travelling show and its English players maintain a certain studied indifference to their precise location throughout, concerned as they are with the eternal verities of dramatic art – Shakespeare, in short. But the troupe harbours a Jewish member, who draws the anti-Semitic wrath of the locals when he engages in an affair with a young Irish girl. The war is imported into the context of the play through the troubled personal history of this character, Rabe; but it is also given an Irish dimension by the manoeuvrings of the Local Defence Force, headed up by the town's baker, Bun Bourke. When he changes costume and puts on his quasi-Nazi gear, Bun's tones become more authoritarian, and the incipient

---

[7] Thomas Kilroy, *Double Cross* (Oldcastle, Co. Meath: Gallery Press, 1994), pp. 88-9.
[8] Kilroy, *Madame MacAdam*, p. 1.

fascism of an Ireland which stayed out of the war is now fully confronted and acknowledged. Jim Nolan's production for Field Day had great fun with the theatrical antics of the visiting troupe, and the crossing of boundaries between onstage and offstage performativity, but it shied away from exploring the darker aspects of such transgressive border crossing in Kilroy's text, and the play itself has yet to receive a definitive production.

What binds together the more recent plays of Thomas Kilroy is their concentration on the figure of the artist. Some of them are well known, such as Oscar Wilde, William Blake; some of them are not, like Nell Jeffrey, the Irish sculptor at the heart of 2003's *The Shape of Metal*. The plays are concerned to show the artist at work, that in Yeats's words 'we must labour to be beautiful', most visually and hence dramatically through Nell's physical labour as she wrests the recalcitrant metal into shape.[9] The play has two time schemes, one when the artist is eighty-two and looks at her hands to remark that they 'couldn't even hold a bloody teacup now'; in other scenes, she is fifty-two and is shown at work welding.[10] But all of these recent artist-centred plays are at pains to convey the dramatic and human truth that artists do not live in romantic isolation, toiling at their masterpieces. There are human connections, and in particular family connections. In *The Secret Fall of Constance Wilde*, so luminously directed at the Abbey in 1997 by Patrick Mason, Oscar Wilde was moved out of the dramatic limelight he so insisted on occupying both on and off the stage and instead dramatic centrality was accorded to his wife, Constance, and their two children. In 'Blake', the space of the artist is shared by his wife Catherine, who provokes him to a self-scrutiny that one senses he is anxious to avoid.[11] It may have seemed to some that Kilroy was according artistic agency to the male, and that women were being demoted to the roles of helpmeet or muse. But social position and dramatic position do not and should not always be automatically equated. Much of the legacy of Ibsen's modernism has been to confer dramatic centrality on a character who is socially confined to playing a subordinate role – quintessentially, Nora in *A Doll's House* – and to explore and to articulate what she suffers by such suppression. Constance Wilde's dramatic importance cannot and

---

[9] W.B. Yeats, 'Adam's Curse', *The Variorum Edition of the Poems of W.B. Yeats*, ed. by Peter Allt and Russell K. Alspach (New York: Macmillan, 1977), p. 205.

[10] Thomas Kilroy, *The Shape of Metal* (Oldcastle, Co. Meath: Gallery Press, 2003), p. 16.

[11] On this, see Anthony Roche's interview with Thomas Kilroy, *Irish University Review* 32:1 (2002), pp. 156-7.

should not be contained and confined within the roles of wife and mother. As Nicky remarks, she protests particularly against the imprisoning role of the 'good woman'.[12] And with *The Shape of Metal* Kilroy creates an impressive and credible woman sculptor in Nell Jeffrey, one who can hold her own in the company (personal and, it is suggested, artistic) of Beckett and Giacometti. Yet her children are no better treated than the families of the male artists. This is particularly the case with Grace, the daughter who has vanished from the 'present' of the play, and so remains the twenty-five-year-old of the flashbacks. Her sister Judith, Nell's other daughter, returns as a woman in her forties to interrogate her mother about their family past and its betrayals. But a second image of Grace does appear in *The Shape of Metal*, not at a particular and different age, but ageless, timeless, as a head sculpted in metal when she was twenty-five. The medium is effaced to show Nell working directly on her daughter's head as her 'busy fingers [are] pressing and shaping, lump of stuff, stone or metal to be transformed into Grace finally at peace, head still and quiet, no terrible dread anymore, no mad panics'.[13]

These late plays are full of the dramatic and damaging encounters between parents and children, not just the fathers and sons of traditional Irish drama, but mothers and daughters, as here. And all three of the characters in *The Secret Fall* – Constance, Oscar and Bosie – have suffered from an oppressive and, to varying degrees, abusive father. If this is the concern of so much Irish drama past and present, Kilroy departs radically from this tradition. Constance Wilde's father is represented by a giant male puppet dressed in Victorian clothes, an all-too-true ogre; her children by puppets manipulated onstage by attendant, anonymous figures. Nell Jeffrey's work as a sculptor and her treatment of her vulnerable daughter are represented by a metallic talking head.

Thomas Kilroy is therefore a modernist writer in an overtly theatrical and self-conscious way. But unlike Beckett, a figure whose art his own resembles and has drawn upon, his theatre does not operate in a deliberately constructed vacuum, a space from which all personal and cultural objects have been removed, torn down or scraped away (even if their traces persist). As Nicky has so persuasively shown, Kilroy's theatre is both theatrically experimental while being 'specifically concerned with the social and political realities of the Ireland in which

---

[12] Thomas Kilroy, *Secret Fall*, p. 13: 'Never again will I be invented as the good woman. Never!'
[13] Kilroy, *Shape of Metal*, p. 11.

he writes'. I did not read Kilroy's essay 'Synge and Modernism' when it was first published in 1972. I was still an undergraduate at Trinity College, Dublin, and, while profoundly influenced by Synge's centenary, my own PhD on J.M. Synge still lay some years in the future. Much of my writing has been about the contemporary Irish stage and Thomas Kilroy's many critical essays on that subject have had a profound impact on my thinking. When much later I read his essay 'Synge the Modernist' I found much to agree with and admire, some of which has been quoted by Nicky. But I was disappointed that, despite the promise of his title, Kilroy instead seemed to view Synge as turning his back on and rejecting 'what is central to European drama of the same period'.[14] This conference and Nicky's paper have led me to re-read the Synge essay more attentively and realize how subtle is its argument. Kilroy shows how Synge appears much more modernist when his plays are not shoehorned within the narrow confines of the early Irish Dramatic Movement. I would agree with that and say further that Synge's plays embody a kind of Irish Modernism which can more readily be seen as an alternative to, rather than a rejection of, the European model. Kilroy's comments in this early essay are most fascinating when they are applied not to Synge's tragically truncated career but to his own achievement of the past forty-plus years. Kilroy has reversed the emphasis: he is a modernist first and Irish second, following on from his great Irish predecessors, explicitly and unequivocally opening up Irish society to the full impact of a European range of sensibility and representation.

---

[14] ibid., p. 167.

Fig. 1 Cover and centre pages of programme for *The Death and Resurrection of Mr. Roche*, Abbey Theatre, Dublin, 1973

Fig. 2 Tom (Jordan) Murphy, Clive Geraghty, and Ray McBride in *The Death and Resurrection of Mr. Roche* by Thomas Kilroy, Abbey Theatre, 1989. Photo: Amelia Stein

Fig. 3 Stephen Brennan, John Molloy, Clive Geraghty, Ingrid Craigie (kneeling) and Eileen Colgan in *Talbot's Box* by Thomas Kilroy, Peacock Theatre, 1977. Photo: Fergus Bourke

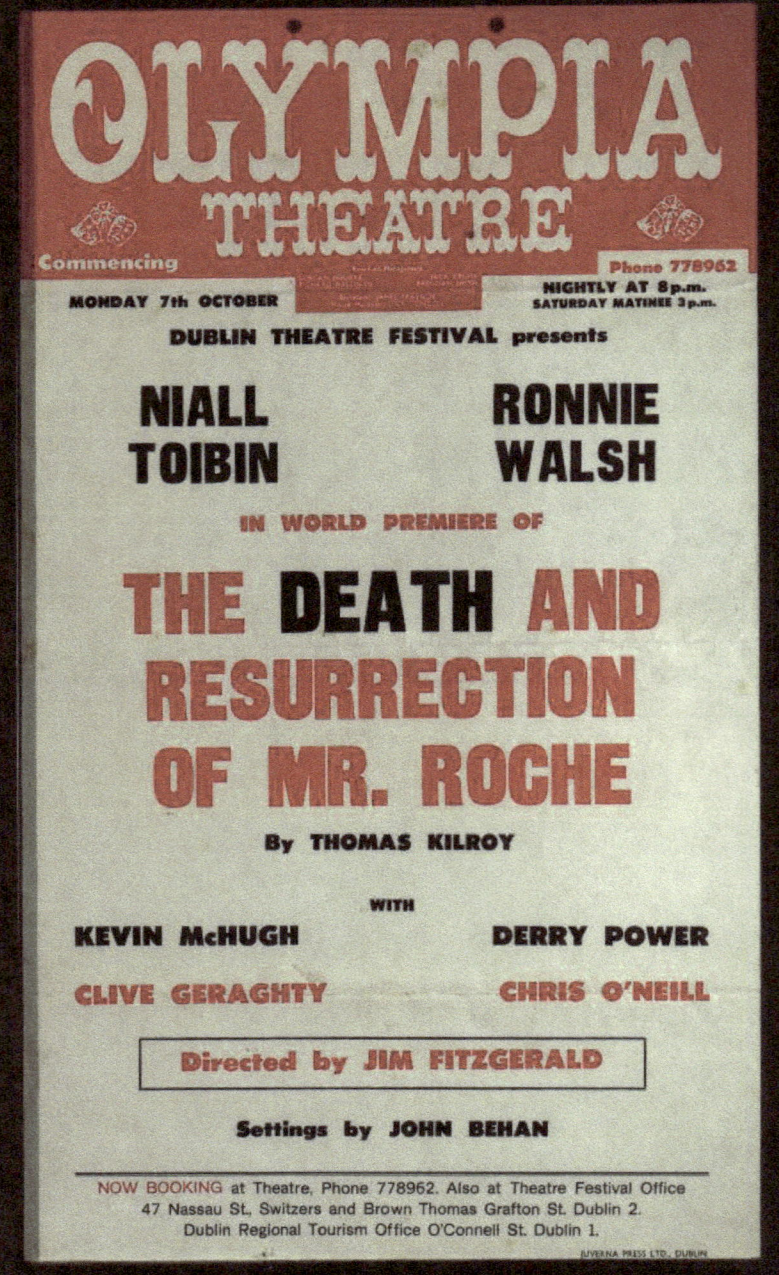

Fig. 4 Poster for *The Death and Resurrection of Mr. Roche*. Olympia Theatre, Dublin, 1968

Fig. 5 Jane Brennan, Kevin Murphy, and Robert O'Mahoney in *The Secret Fall of Constance Wilde* by Thomas Kilroy, Abbey Theatre, 1997.
Photo: Amelia Stein

Fig. 6 Cover of programme for *Tea and Sex and Shakespeare*, Rough Magic Theatre Company, 1988

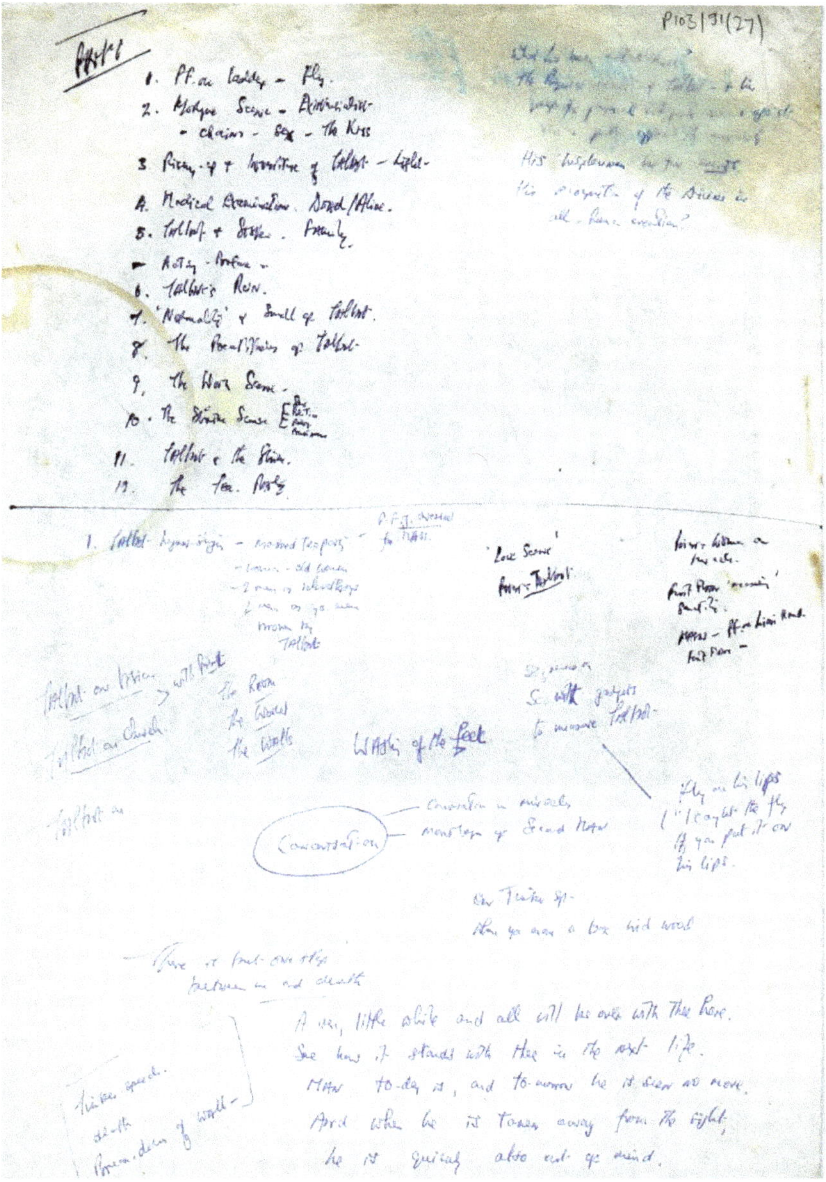

Fig. 7 Thomas Kilroy, notes for *Talbot's Box*

Fig. 8 Aoife Duffin in *Christ Deliver Us!*, Abbey Theatre 2010.
Photo: Ros Kavanagh

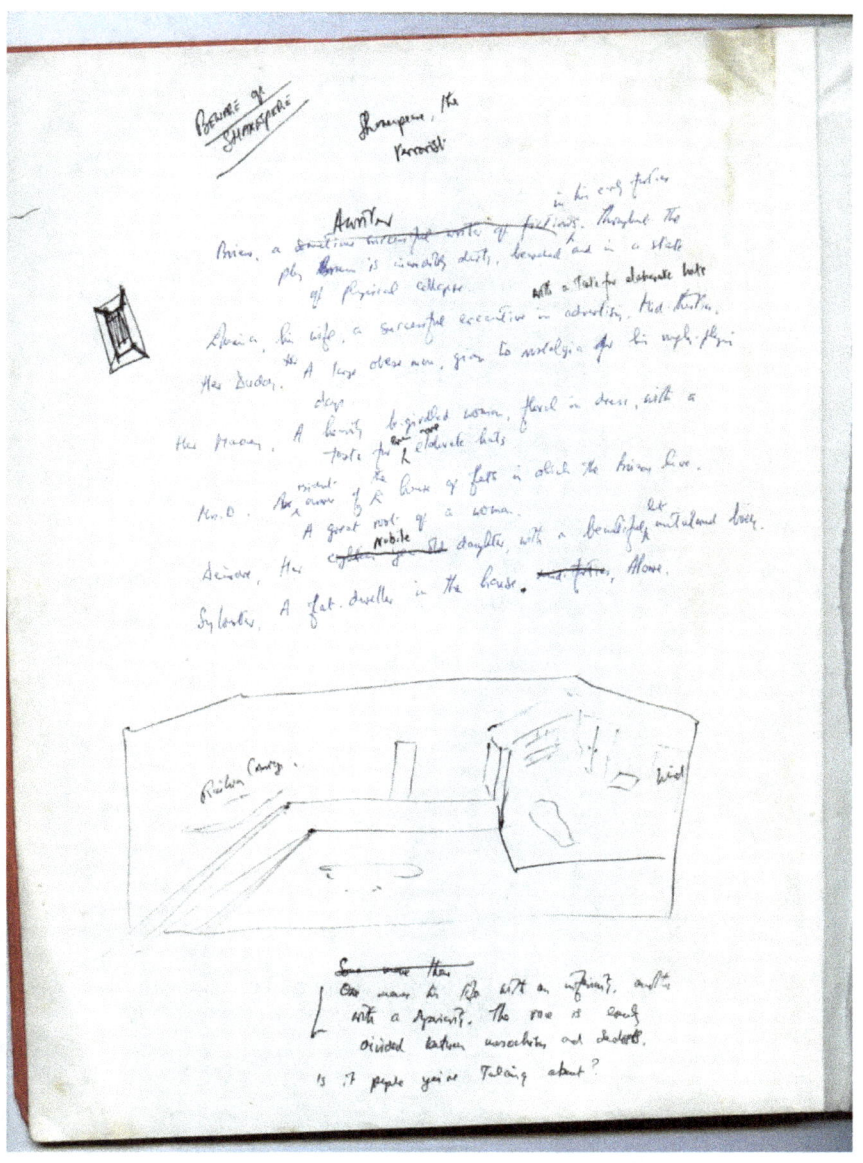

Fig. 9 Thomas Kilroy, notes for *Tea and Sex and Shakespeare*

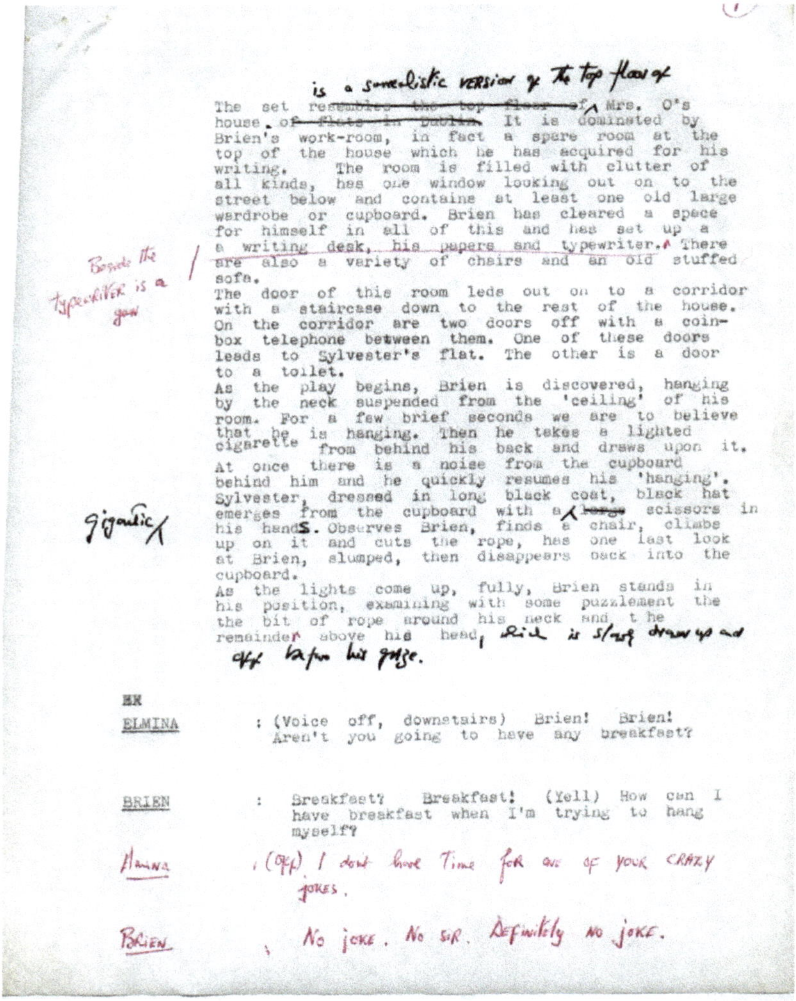

The set ~~resembles the top floor of~~ is a surrealistic version of the top floor of Mrs. O's house ~~of flats in Dublin~~. It is dominated by Brien's work-room, in fact a spare room at the top of the house which he has acquired for his writing. The room is filled with clutter of all kinds, has one window looking out on to the street below and contains at least one old large wardrobe or cupboard. Brien has cleared a space for himself in all of this and has set up a writing desk, his papers and typewriter. [Beside the typewriter is a gun] There are also a variety of chairs and an old stuffed sofa.

The door of this room leads out on to a corridor with a staircase down to the rest of the house. On the corridor are two doors off with a coin-box telephone between them. One of these doors leads to Sylvester's flat. The other is a door to a toilet.

As the play begins, Brien is discovered, hanging by the neck suspended from the 'ceiling' of his room. For a few brief seconds we are to believe that he is hanging. Then he takes a lighted cigarette from behind his back and draws upon it. At once there is a noise from the cupboard behind him and he quickly resumes his 'hanging'. Sylvester, dressed in long black coat, black hat emerges from the cupboard with a [gigantic] ~~huge~~ scissors in his hands. Observes Brien, finds a chair, climbs up on it and cuts the rope, has one last look at Brien, slumped, then disappears back into the cupboard.

As the lights come up, fully, Brien stands in his position, examining with some puzzlement the bit of rope around his neck and the remainder above his head, and is slung drawn up and off taken his gaze.

ELMINA : (Voice off, downstairs) Brien! Brien! Aren't you going to have any breakfast?

BRIEN : Breakfast? Breakfast! (Yell) How can I have breakfast when I'm trying to hang myself?

ELMINA : (off) I don't have time for one of your crazy jokes.

BRIEN : No joke. No sir. Definitely no joke.

Fig. 10 Thomas Kilroy, typescript and revisions to *Tea and Sex and Shakespeare*

Fig. 11 Cover of programme for *The Death and Resurrection of Mr. Roche*, Hampstead Theatre Club, London, 1969

4 | The Intellectual on Stage

Thomas Kilroy

This is an attempt to say something about three Anglo-Irish playwrights whose work displays intellectuality, admittedly in very different ways, Beckett, Yeats and George Bernard Shaw. I am going to work backwards, from Beckett to Yeats and Yeats to Shaw, to try to illustrate what has been eliminated in Beckett: the social, the cultural, the representational, the reflection on stage of life outside the theatre. Shaw may be seen as the naturalist, the social realist of the three, but what is not often acknowledged is that, in this context, the attempt to escape from naturalistic theatre begins with Shaw in his later plays. The experiments there may not always work but the movement is towards fantasy and the surreal and the movement is intellectual.

In this discussion the quality of mind of the playwright is at least as important as the stage action, that which is being dramatized upon the stage. In fact, the two are inextricable and what is being dramatized, permeating everything else, is the mind of the playwright in action.

This is a problematical area. Firstly, there is the problem of commerce and the fact that the intellectual playwright cannot be marketed. At the other end of the spectrum there is the conviction that the more visceral, the more spontaneous, the more unmediated the theatrical experience, the better. From this perspective intellectuality may appear to be a brake or block on creativity itself.

Theatre, too, is a collaborative art form in ways in which other art forms are not. Without the group there can be no theatre. Intellectual expression has to find its place in that group, if it is to survive. So, whatever else we are talking about here we are not talking about the intellectual as theorist, the intellectual as essayist. In other words we are not talking about the common expression of the intellectual which is the imposition of a strong, single vision upon others, inviting response, yes, but with absolute conviction as to the validity of its own argument. I see intellectuality in the theatre as different, less dictatorial, as something which takes its place, along with other kinds of expression, in a larger scheme of things.

There is one other feature of drama which may pose a conflict between intellectuality and staging. Drama is most often best served by direct simplicity, simplicity of form, simplicity of idea. Abstracted from even the most complex plays, this central idea may be expressed in a simple formula, what Yeats called 'the single effect'. Someone once said of Shaw that each of his plays could be reduced to a single epigram. There is an implied conflict here between simplicity of form and complexity of thought which is one of the technical problems which faced each of these three playwrights.

The usual exploration of the intellect, on the other hand, doesn't always work in this way, through simplicity. The pull is in a different direction not towards limiting the idea but towards its exhaustion in a growing density of meaning and an accumulating assembly of references. There are commentators, for instance, who would say that the expression of ideas in drama is necessarily superficial, that the intellectual burden of a play cannot be anything more than what an audience can absorb quickly and in a brief time span.

If all of this sounds problematical, what of the intellectual writer's response to it? Certainly there is a defensiveness on the part of some playwrights who feel the need to provide elaborate exegesis of their work in the form of explanatory essays. Shaw's vast body of prefaces is one example of this and it is clear from the importance which he attached to these prefaces that he considered them to be an intrinsic part of the plays themselves. Yeats, on the other hand, displays an admirable loftiness on the subject of the intellectual content of his plays. Intelligence, for Yeats, never needed a defence. But the most graphic example of an intellectual reaction of a playwright towards critical debate on his work is to be found in Beckett.

Beckett had a kind of wild comic method of dealing with questions of an intellectual nature in relation to his work. In the early 1950s he wrote two letters which illustrate this, one written just before, and one just after the initial appearance on stage in Paris of *Waiting for Godot*.

The first letter was to Michel Polac who was planning a broadcast of extracts from the play to try to promote a full scale, stage production. This was the great age of radio drama when a writer like Ionescu could make his first appearance in English not on stage but over the air waves. The radio production of *Waiting for Godot*, it was hoped, might expedite a stage production, which is, in fact, what happened.

The second letter was to the director of the first German production of the play, Carlheinz Caspari, when Beckett had already had the experience of seeing the play in performance in Paris. Both letters are typical of the exchanges which take place between a playwright and director of new work but with this difference: Beckett is wholly anarchic on the subject of theatre. In answer to a query about his idea of theatre, he says that he is completely ignorant about theatre because he never goes to it. He goes on to say that he knows nothing about *Waiting for Godot* itself, that he is deeply suspicious of anyone who tries to find meaning in it and that he resists, strongly, any efforts at analysis of what is going on up on that stage.

There is, of course, a reason for such a strategy. Beckett was determined that his play reach its audience without interpretation, that the experience in the theatre be a frontal one of engagement with the thing itself, no more, no less. Something begins, something proceeds, something ends. Above all he resists the notion of theatre as representation. This does not represent something else, it is, to paraphrase Beckett himself on the subject of *Finnegans Wake*, it is the thing itself.

Here is the spare account of this from the first letter, the one to Polac:

> I know no more about this play than anyone who manages to read it attentively.
> I do not know in what spirit I wrote it.
> I know no more of the characters than what they say, what they do and what happens to them. Of their appearance, I must have indicated the little I have been able to make out. The bowler hats for example.
> I do not know who Godot is. I do not even know if he exists. And I do not know if they believe he does, these two who are waiting for him.[1]

By disowning knowledge Beckett would appear to have divested himself of all intellectual intention in his play. But then, towards the end of the letter, he reveals his choice of positioning which is at the centre of much intellectuality in theatre, that is, distancing, the cool

---

[1] Letter from Samuel Beckett to Michel Polac, after 23 January 1952, *The Letters of Samuel Beckett Volume II: 1941-1956*, ed. George Craig, Martha Dow Fehsenfeld, Dan Gunn and Lois More Overbeck (Cambridge: Cambridge University Press, 2011), pp. 314-17 (p. 316).

removal of the author from the subject matter, the rising above the actual, the particular, to a position of supremely distanced perspective, in other words to a position of intellectual possession, intellectual shaping of the material. The position which Beckett achieves is an intellectual one which gives him apparent freedom from thought itself. But if he arrives at this post-intellectual status, beyond the process of thought, he can only have arrived there by a profound process of thinking.

This distancing in Beckett is close to Yeats's discovery of Asiatic simplicity of staging and its distancing from the need to represent something outside the theatre:

> I hope to have attained the distance from life which can make credible strange events, elaborate words. I have written a little play that can be played in a room [...] There will be no scenery.[2]

This is also the stance which draws much of the hostility to ideas in the theatre, the unwarranted claim that the intellectual is too remote and lacking in feeling. This is simply a failure to recognize the depth of passion which can be conveyed through thinking. Here is Beckett again from that perch above the created play:

> I am no longer part of it, and never will be again. Estragon, Vladimir, Pozzo and Lucky, their time and space, I have been able to know a little about them by staying very far away from the need to understand.[3]

In his second letter, the one to the German director, on the identity of Godot, he offers one of those dizzy, comic turns of his: 'If [Godot's] name suggests the heavens, it is only to the extent that a product to promote hair growth can seem heavenly'.[4]

One of the hazards facing the intellectual in writing a play is the temptation to intervene, to interpolate ideas into the script, to editorialize or otherwise express ideas that haven't earned their places in the action of the play. There are a couple of such moments in *Waiting for Godot* which raise this issue, and it is worth reflecting on how Beckett triumphs over the problem.

---

[2] W.B. Yeats, 'Certain Noble Plays of Japan', in *The Collected Works of W.B. Yeats Volume IV: Early Essays*, ed. George Bornstein and Richard J. Finneran (New York: Scribner, 2007) pp. 163-73 (p. 163).
[3] Beckett to Michel Polac, after 23 January 1952, *Letters of Samuel Beckett Volume II*, p. 316.
[4] Beckett to Carlheinz Caspari, 25 July 1953, *Letters of Samuel Beckett Volume II*, pp. 388-93 (p. 391).

One is Lucky's monologue in Act One, a savage, ironical display of the futility of all reasoning. Another is Vladimir's beautiful threnody with its dying fall towards the end of the play:

> Was I sleeping while the others suffered? Am I sleeping now? Tomorrow, when I wake, or think I do, what shall I say of today? That with Estragon my friend, at this place, until the fall of night, I waited for Godot? That Pozzo passed, with his carrier, and that he spoke to us? Probably. But in all that what truth will there be?[5]

In addition to these two interventions, a possible third is Pozzo's distraught outburst on 'accursed time', but that particular moment is more integrated into the preceding dialogue. The other two are different; they are surprising eruptions on the surface of banality and routine, moments of intense focus or anchorage in a flow of disconnectedness and absurdity, moments, in other words, where the mind of the author is fully on display.

By freeing the stage of representation Beckett gave himself immense freedom to surprise his audience. Surprise and the unexpected are ancient ingredients of theatre. In Beckett the surprises are intellectual, freed of the tyranny of knowledge and of the obligations of narrative.

There is a difficulty here for the actor. Actors like to find what they call 'lines' in a play's development, for instance lines in character development, which allow them to build towards particular moments of intensity. They are uncomfortable with moments of intensity which appear to come out of nowhere. But Beckett's creatures are not characters in the conventional sense. They are usable figures in a setting which retains its staginess throughout. The stage remains a stage even after the first line is spoken, after the first steps have been taken from point A to point B.

In his letter to Caspari Beckett himself was perfectly aware of this difficulty for the actor and director but he was also intellectually secure in his own ambitions. He is adamant that this is not a symbolist play nor is it a play of forms and ideas: 'First and foremost it is a question of something that happens, almost a routine, and it is this dayliness and this materiality, in my view that needs to be brought out'. On characterization he provides a breathtaking, intellectual lucidity that in one move undermines the whole, traditional idea of human identity on the stage:

---

[5] Samuel Beckett, *Waiting for Godot*, in *The Complete Dramatic Works* (London: Faber and Faber, 1986), pp. 7-88 (p. 84).

> The characters are living creatures, only just living perhaps, they are not emblems. I can readily understand your unease at their lack of characterization. But I would urge you to see in them less the result of an attempt at abstraction, something I am almost incapable of, than a refusal to tone down all that is at one and the same time complex and amorphous in them.[6]

Then, like an afterthought, he offers the fortunate German director a consolation derived from his own experience of seeing the first production in Paris and in doing so he restores the creatures of his imagination to the human family. 'If I may judge from our experience here in Paris, you will see identities shaping up as your work proceeds'.[7]

To move back from Beckett to Yeats and Shaw is to observe something of what Beckett has eliminated including the conventional idea of characterization. He had his own opinions of Yeats and Shaw, a huge respect for the poet and a less than positive view of Shaw. In yet another letter, on June 1st 1956, he responded to a request from the Irish actor Cyril Cusack to write a programme note, in French, no less, on Shaw, for a production at the Gaiety Theatre in Dublin. He puts Yeats, Synge and even O'Casey ahead of Shaw. Here is his response to Cusack's request:

> This is too tall an order for me. I wouldn't write in French for King's Street. I wouldn't suggest that GBS is not a great playwright, whatever that is when it's at home. What I would do is give the whole unupsettable apple-cart for a sup of the Hawk's Well, or the Saints', or a whiff of Juno, to go no further.[8]

In truth all three of these playwrights are engaged in the elimination of naturalistic detail in order to clear space for the expression of intellect. Beckett is engaged in the elimination of received myth, which Yeats drew upon so heavily, replacing it with personal myth, a mythology of emptiness for the mid-twentieth-century. Yeats, too, is engaged in the elimination of the naturalism which Shaw was so dependent on at the start of his career. 'I have been thinking a good deal about plays lately', Yeats wrote in 1903, 'and I have been wondering why I dislike the clear and logical construction which seems necessary if

---

[6] Beckett to Carlheinz Caspari, 25 July 1953, *Letters of Samuel Beckett Volume II*, p. 391.
[7] ibid.
[8] Beckett to Cyril Cusack, 1 June 1956, *Letters of Samuel Beckett Volume II*, p. 623.

one is to succeed on the modern stage'.[9] You feel that he has to be thinking of the great success of Shaw: remember the nightmare which he had of Shaw appearing to him as a knitting machine in perpetual motion.

But Shaw, too, as he proceeded, tried to shift drama into a new dimension as he does in Act Three of *Man and Superman* or in later plays like *Too True to be Good*. The latter anticipated, and perhaps even influenced, later theatrical developments in the twentieth century.

In each of the three cases the aim is the same: to divest the stage of the furniture of the ordinary to create a free stage space to release the free play of intelligence. This free stage space is given meaning, not by reference to life off-stage but by the nature of events that happen on-stage, as in the startling lines setting the scene of Yeats's play *The Herne's Egg*:

> This is Tara; in a moment
> Men must come out of the gate.[10]

Like Beckett, Yeats considered conventional characterization an obstacle to this free expression. One can see why. The illusion of traditional characterization in the theatre is that we have before us a complex individuality, which includes the illusion of independence, independent, that is, of its author. Traditional characterization has the waywardness of real life, its unpredictability, with opinions that seem to arise out of the individuality of the character and not as a mouthpiece of the author.

In order to deal with this Yeats worked out a theory of stage characterization. It arises from his reflecting on the critical dogma 'that if a play does not contain definite character, its constitution is not strong enough for the stage'.[11] He then, as always, goes back into the tradition of drama where he suddenly finds illumination:

> Suddenly it strikes us that character is continuously present in comedy alone, and there is much tragedy, that of Corneille, Racine, that of Greece and Rome, where its place is taken by passions and motives, one person being jealous, another full of love or remorse or pride or anger.[12]

---

[9] Yeats, 'Emotion of Multitude' in *Collected Works of W.B. Yeats Volume IV*, pp. 159-61 (p. 159).
[10] W.B. Yeats, *The Herne's Egg* in *Selected Plays*, ed. Richard Allen Cave (London: Penguin, 1997), pp. 229-54 (p. 238).
[11] Yeats, 'The Tragic Theatre' in *Collected Works of W.B. Yeats Volume IV*, pp. 174-79 (p. 175).
[12] ibid.

Passion, for Yeats, removes the tragic character from the attendant details of characterization, to a place of stillness and silence, of what he calls 'tragic reverie' where passion becomes wisdom, disembodied, beyond time. It is remarkable how often Yeats anticipates Beckett, as in his account of this tragic suspension portrayed in great painting 'where we find there sadness and gravity, a certain emptiness even, as of a mind that waited the supreme crisis (and indeed it seems at times as if the graphic art, unlike poetry which sings the crisis itself, were the celebration of waiting)'.[13]

As we know, at a certain point Yeats withdrew altogether from public theatre, retreating to a form of private drama 'distinguished, indirect, and symbolic, and having no need of mob or Press to pay its way – an aristocratic form'.[14] There are many possible responses to this, including outright rejection. But if we stay with Yeats on his own terms we see an achievement of bold intellectual ambition. One of the clearest descriptions of how this private drama might be presented is in the opening stage directions of the play *The Resurrection*.

> Before I had finished this play I saw that its subject-matter might make it unsuited for the public stage in England or Ireland. I had begun it with an ordinary stage scene in the mind's eye, curtained walls, a window and door at back, a curtained door at left. I now changed the stage directions and wrote songs for the unfolding and folding of the curtain that it might be played in a studio or a drawing-room like my dance plays, or at the Peacock Theatre before a specially chosen audience.[15]

In this short one act play Yeats dramatizes nothing less than the collision of Christianity and Graeco-Roman civilization. In the 1931 edition of the play his usable figures are labelled The Hebrew, The Syrian and The Greek, representing the three main currents of early western civilization. These are the carriers of the play's action, the voices who carry the interpreting intelligence behind the play.

If this were a play by Shaw we would have been offered a triangular debate between the three figures, on the nature of progress, perhaps, or on what constitutes the exceptional individual, the kind of person who makes a significant contribution to the evolution of the species. While Yeats's play is also highly verbal it goes beyond language to ritual. The

---

[13] ibid., p. 178.
[14] Yeats, 'Certain Noble Plays of Japan', in *Collected Works of W.B. Yeats Volume IV*, p. 163.
[15] Yeats, *The Resurrection* in *Selected Plays*, pp. 193-204 (p. 193).

three figures enact a ritual of revelation, revelation of the violent, bloody moment which, in the Yeatsian vision, marks one cycle of history from another. This is the killing of a god and the consuming of his flesh and blood. Yeats was fascinated by such mystery-cults, seeing the Christian myth as part of the myths of death and resurrection of the cults of the dying god, Attis, Adonis or Dionysus, devoured by his followers. His play ends with the apparition of the risen god with its beating heart. Belief in the supernatural is what, finally, distinguishes the Yeatsian theatre from that of Beckett and Shaw.

Even in the most Beckettian of these short plays of Yeats, *Purgatory*, the distinction from Beckett is pronounced. Many people have remarked upon how the play anticipates Beckett in the achieved simplicity of the figures in the scene: an old man, a boy, a ruined house, a bare tree. The profound difference, however, is that Yeats relies upon a complex, specific idea, that of cyclical repetition in life which imprisons the human as did the old device of Fate. Beckett freed himself from all such specifics.

The standard account of Shaw's development as a playwright would say that he begins as a nineteenth-century Ibsenite with the so-called problem or discussion plays like *Widowers' Houses* and *Mrs Warren's Profession*. Later he tried to move away from naturalism and sociology to a theatre of personal vision. Throughout, however, the essential Shavian stage device is the dramatic debate, a dialectic in which the process of thesis and antithesis is at least as important as synthesis, if there is one, 'changing us', as Shaw put it, 'from bewildered spectators of a monstrous confusion to men intelligently conscious of the world and its destinies'.[16] He believed that this intellectual conversion, as it were, of the audience is the true business of the great playwrights whom he lists from Euripides to Ibsen. No doubt he would have included himself on the list.

One of the turning points in this development of Shaw is the third act of *Man and Superman*. The single, simple theatrical formula which Shaw returns to again and again is that of romantic comedy, the journey of a couple or couples towards marriage or the prospect of marriage, overcoming comic obstacles along the way, the most important one being inadequate self-knowledge. John Tanner and Ann Whitefield in *Man and Superman* fulfil this role with this crucial addition. Because they are creatures of what Shaw called the 'Life Force' they are swept by

---

[16] George Bernard Shaw, 'Preface to Three Plays by Brieux', in *The Complete Prefaces Volume I: 1889-1913*, ed. Dan H. Laurence and Daniel J. Leary (London: Allen Lane, The Penguin Press, 1993), pp. 531-65 (p. 544).

a power in nature that is greater than any human agency. The traditional, romantic-comic surrender of male to female or female to male at the end of this play becomes a powerful collapse which has some semblance to death. When Ann says to Tanner in that strange conclusion of their romance 'you very nearly killed me, Jack', she means it.[17]

Shaw subtitled the play, ominously, 'A Comedy and a Philosophy'. The philosophy comes mostly in Act Three of the play, where he transposes his finely detailed social drama into the hereafter, a benign hell of almost endless intellectual discussion complete with an easily offended Lucifer. All this is accomplished on stage with the aid of the new-fangled machine, the motor car. There are four characters. Tanner becomes Don Juan, Ann becomes Doña Ana and her father has been transmogrified into a talking statue. The fourth character, the devil, is Tanner's antagonist in the debate, but Ann and her father participate as well. The subjects covered in this most overt form of intellectual theatre include Heaven and Hell, obviously, the place of culture in English society, human evolution and the Life Force, militarism, the works of Dante and Milton, gender and civilization, together with several asides of a critical nature on the arts. It is a relentless assault on the patience of its audience. Far from Beckett and Yeats the specific ideas rain down upon the stage and even the devil complains about the length of the speeches.

It would be easy to conclude that this intellectuality of debating in Shaw is of a lesser order than the intellectuality of Yeats or Beckett, more mechanical, less subtle, more prosaic, less poetical. But it is also important to acknowledge that Shaw in his own way is also a visionary. This vision, too, is intellectual. *Too True to Be Good* opens with a patient in bed (and this is how she is referred to throughout, as the Patient). By the bedside sits a huge microbe of luminous jelly which looks like a monster from a science-fiction film. The microbe takes a lively part in the satirical, medical bedside scene that follows. The play itself is an angry, prophetic, apocalyptic, disillusioned drama masquerading as whimsical comedy. It reflects the deep disturbance in Europe between the wars. The comedy, like that of Beckett, is often close to despair. The problem with the play, like the late Shaw plays generally, is that, despite the surrealism, the science fiction, the fantasy, you feel Shaw never fully surrenders to the radical theatricality that he

---

[17] George Bernard Shaw, *Man and Superman: A Comedy and a Philosophy*, in *The Bodley Head Bernard Shaw Volume II* (London: The Bodley Head, 1971), pp. 533-733 (p. 731).

is toying with. His consuming interest in society is still here, the comic style is still that of the paradox and the epigram of the early plays and the relentless debates continue on and on like a tic out of control.

Shaw was fully aware, however, of the difficulty of experiment in theatre. At the age of seventy-nine he talked about the member of the audience in a programme note, as follows:

> He must be prepared to come across from time to time a sort of play which quite upsets his notions of what a play should be. He may not like it at first, but if it takes a grip of the stage, he must go on enduring it until he does like it.[18]

He was defending his own late plays here but he might also have been addressing the troubled first audiences of *Waiting for Godot*, twenty years later, in Paris.

[This is an edited text of the Madden-Rooney Public Lecture delivered at the University of Notre Dame, Dublin Seminar, 14 June 2012. It was first published in *Irish Pages: A Journal of Contemporary Writing* (Vol. 7 No. 2, 2013).]

---

[18] George Bernard Shaw, 'The Simple Truth of the Matter', epilogue to *The Simpleton of the Unexpected Isles: A Vision of Judgment*, in *The Bodley Head Bernard Shaw Volume VI* (London: The Bodley Head, 1973), pp. 841-46 (p. 842).

5 | Publishing Plays and the Plays of Thomas Kilroy

Peter Fallon

In April 2011, Trinity College Dublin conferred on Thomas Kilroy an honorary fellowship for his 'role in shaping Irish theatre'. This (and the various other distinctions that have come his way) was truly earned and richly deserved. But I've found myself wondering about that word 'shaping', a word which conjures of course the title of one of his most interesting plays, *The Shape of Metal*. And I've been wondering because I suspect that if the author of that brief citation were to elaborate on it, he or she would quickly find him or herself qualifying it. If 'shape' is an external form or appearance characteristic of something, or the outline of an area, or – we might say – a fixed, definite or orderly arrangement of that area, I wonder if it isn't truer to suggest that Thomas Kilroy's ever and still-evolving art isn't a *defiance* of shape, in any settled or completed sense, in favour of a constant *shape*-shifting, and, both in his own plays and in his ideas about drama, a redefinition of our theatre. This is but one of the qualities and instructions that have attracted me to his work and to my involvement in its publication for more than thirty years.

Let me digress and express what I think is a common perception – that is, that Gallery is thought of first as a poetry-publishing enterprise. Fair enough. It's true that most of the nearly five hundred titles we've issued have been poetry editions. But in the course of almost forty years, we've published what I'd like to think of as a library of eighty plays by our finest playwrights, Thomas Kilroy, Brian Friel, Tom Murphy, Eugene McCabe, Stewart Parker, Jim Nolan, Marina Carr and, in Irish, Brendan Behan. That list contains some of the great plays of the last half century and is a fair sampler of the western dramatic tradition, including as it does, besides original plays, adaptations and translations by playwrights and poets – and a novelist – of works by

Sophocles and Aristophanes, Racine, Molière and Rostand. We've also published what its author, John Banville, calls 'a contradiction in terms', that is, a German comedy, as well as other plays by Kleist, by Ibsen, Turgenev, and of course Chekhov, and, more recently, in the masterful re-imaginings of Kilroy, by Wedekind and Pirandello.

So what fuels a perhaps perilous taking-for-granted of such a list? I think it's a belief, shared by people closer to the inner workings of theatre, that the play, by which they mean the staged play, is the thing, and in fact is the only thing. I know I've read more plays than I've seen, that I've read plays in translations I wouldn't understand in the original, and that I've found this fulfilling, enlightening, entertaining, moving and, well, enough. I suppose this is a way of owning up to an interest, first, in what might be called 'literary' drama, and it is because of the excitements and satisfactions of that involvement in the publishing of Thomas Kilroy's plays that it pleased me to be asked to speak today about publishing plays and, in particular, the shock of publishing the plays of Thomas Kilroy.

I was a student at Trinity when I started publishing Gallery books. They were, at first, books of poems by young writers. Before long I was publishing two of my teachers, Brendan Kennelly, already established as one of Ireland's leading and beloved writers, and Eiléan Ní Chuilleanáin, whose first book of poems I published in 1972. (I've mentioned elsewhere the thought that this might be a clever move, and might help with my grades. I was wrong. Again.) But while I was trying to write my own poems and had a calling to the publication of those by other people, my interest in drama persisted. My first steps in publishing plays, however, were less professional than personal. It happened in the summer of 1974 that I was, you might say, courting an actress who, that September, played the lead role in a one-act play that started its life in the Project Theatre, then in South King Street, and continued its run via the Peacock to the Abbey stage. That play was called *On the Outside*, and being close to my friend I first got close to the inner machinery of a play's production. I remember saying to her one night at the end of its successful run: 'Now what happens to it? It simply disappears?' That didn't seem right, but it could be put right.

On the Outside by Tom Murphy and Noel O'Donoghue, with its companion piece *On the Inside*, were the first plays that Gallery published, and I remember clearly the look on the face of one Mrs Murnane, the Irish buyer in Hodges Figgis, at that time on the other side of Dawson Street, when I told her my plan. Publishing poetry is one thing, she said, with a shake of her head, clearly thinking it a foolishness that could be entertained, but plays? That was beyond the wildest stretch of her reason. Nobody buys plays in Ireland, I was told. They can't, I thought, nobody publishes them.

So within a couple of years I'd enlisted plays I'd not seen but which were still talked about, which I read and admired – plays such as Eugene McCabe's *King of the Castle*, Heno Magee's *Hatchet*, Tom Murphy's *Famine*, and, in due course, his *A Whistle in the Dark*. And then, in October 1977, I had the good fortune to be one of the few who attended what was the premiere of *Talbot's Box*, under Patrick Mason's sure, steadying, brave and, now that I come to think of it, very young hand. It was, of course, a marvel. Enthralled and transported, it struck me as only one other play had affected me up to that time, and that was the play we were hauled to in Limerick, from my boarding school nearby. I was fourteen and the play was *The Field*, with Ray McAnally as the 'Bull' McCabe. As we say, I couldn't believe what we were seeing and hearing, but, in truth, I couldn't but believe it. Not that we knew people like John B. Keane's characters, but we knew of people like them: they lived down the lanes and off the main roads surrounding the home place in County Meath, where they lived in stories we heard, or perhaps more properly, not in stories we heard but in stories we overheard.

That jolt of recognition, and the forceful potential of drama, marked me like a brand. (Next day, incidentally, McAnally and other members of the travelling troupe came to speak to us in Glenstal. I got the impression then that has intrigued me often since: they weren't as interesting in life as they'd been on the stage.) Different and all as Keane's realism is from *Talbot's Box*, the impacts of these plays were similar, and when we came to publish the latter there was a phrase in Thomas Kilroy's introductory essay that has stayed with me as suggestive as something central to his preoccupations. The play is a study of Matt Talbot, 'the workers' saint', pitched against seismic moments in Dublin's history – the 'lock out' of 1913, the Rising of three years later, and the atmosphere of Ireland's fledgling independence. But more than the outward life, albeit with its devotion to prayer, penance and fasting, Kilroy foregrounds a notion of the secret life of the mystic working man at the play's core. And it's that secret life that he returns to again and again, and explores in other characters. (And, of course, that word recurs in the title of his play about Mrs Wilde, *The Secret Fall of Constance Wilde*.) For all of *Talbot's Box*'s visionary soar and reach towards transcendence, for all of its theatrical innovation and adventure, its final speech endures as one of the most gorgeous pieces of writing we've ever published, in almost five hundred titles over the course of more than forty years.

So the series of plays that we'd taken to publishing was up and running, and it gathered speed and momentum and new status the year that we published Thomas Kilroy's first Gallery play. It was then that I was bold enough to write to one of our heroes, Brian Friel, to tell him what we were doing – I'm sure Brian knew what we were doing, Brian knows everything – and to ask if he might have something we could publish. He offered an early play he said he'd a fondness for, and proposed that we issue a selection of his stories, long out of print. I grabbed both offers, and since then I've published more than a score of other titles, most of them on their opening nights in the Gate and Abbey. That, too, has been a crucial and most rewarding facet of my time as a publisher.

But somehow and for some reason, while *Talbot's Box* remained in print for many years, we didn't publish Kilroy's newer plays, and I have to admit I don't know why. But I do know the shock one day, a dozen years after we published it, when I was thinking about a reprint and I broadened my thought to wonder about other plays of Kilroy's we might make available through publication. Here was someone we spoke of as one of our leading writers, whose plays had won prizes and had been the successes of major festivals, whose first novel had won the *Guardian* prize and the Royal Society of Literature's Heinemann Award, whose plays had been published by Faber and Faber and Methuen, and here was the shock: he was one of our leading writers, a man in his fifties, and not one of his books was in print, not one. Now if a shock is a sudden upsetting, or a surprising experience, that's what I felt, and I also felt some guilt. If an electrical shock is a discharge of power through the body that derives from contact with or exposure to a live current, what I realized in a second was that something simply wasn't right, but, that again, it could be put right. There and then I proposed to Tom that we publish everything, all of the plays, in uniform editions. From that first mention of a Kilroy 'programme', I foresaw a problem. Later we met a roadblock. But we committed anyway to that programme and started to issue a number of plays that had never been between covers: his first stage play, *The O'Neill*, a revised version of *Tea and Sex and Shakespeare*, and others such as *Double Cross*, his first Field Day play, when Faber and Faber let the rights lapse. (Let me interject a particular interest in this play, *Double Cross*. From my first hearing that Thomas Kilroy was writing a play about William Joyce, or 'Lord Haw Haw' as he was called, I felt a distantly personal connection to its subject, because I'd always grown up with the knowledge that, when Joyce was being hunted and was shot before his arrest, four times in the buttocks actually, it was my uncle, Martin Fallon, who operated on him and, even, it's recorded, refused to release him to the authorities until his wounds had healed sufficiently. That, you understand, was in the determination that Joyce would be in the full flower of health when they took him to hang him shortly afterwards.)

And then loomed the problem I'd foreseen. When I said I'd publish everything I wondered how I'd deal with, or accommodate in our list, *The Death and Resurrection of Mr. Roche,* a play I'd never seen but which I'd read as a student at this university at a time when I read more of the plays of Harold Pinter than I could stand, and which for years I'd associated with that other playwright's suffocated milieu. But publish it I did: that was part of the promise. It took me years, and not until *Mr. Roche* received a rehearsed reading as part of a Friel-fest in the Abbey in 2009, to see there was more than I had been aware of in it. I learned how moving the play's second act is, and how sympathetically the central character is drawn. Even if we come to them late, such lessons are blessings.

We've published too, Kilroy's great adaptations of works by Ibsen (*Ghosts*) and Chekhov (*The Seagull*) and, on their opening nights, *The Secret Fall of Constance Wilde, The Shape of Metal,* his Wedekind, (*Christ Deliver Us!*), his Pirandellos, and, because we couldn't wait for an opening night, *My Scandalous Life.* That roadblock I mentioned is our failure so far to acquire the rights to *The Madame MacAdam Travelling Theatre,* clung to by its publishers who seem interested in it only because we're interested in it, and which, Tom has told me, he's never seen in a shop.

From my early, privileged readings of scripts, often long before the productions are mooted, I've detected how Kilroy's anatomies of personality, frequently at that moment of collision between self and social pressure, are, essentially, portraits of the artist. And as such, as is so often the case, they are self-portraits too, of an artist in whose care the art is safe. To read these plays is to attend a master-class in the art and its possibilities. For someone like me, who doesn't write plays, his example transmits not as a set of techniques but as a store of values.

Another shock that sometimes precedes publication can also be a jolt of pleasure. The sense of responsibility one has when one is presented with a new manuscript has never left me. In the case of work by those we cherish, those first sentiments of eager anticipation are matched by a nervousness and apprehension that, you hope, will be followed quickly by relief. I remember this most clearly some while after I had to tell another Tom that I wouldn't publish one of his plays. That was a truly awful piece of work, most of which he sang to me on the telephone in an attempt to make me reconsider my decision. Shortly afterwards he showed me another manuscript. That initial nervousness turned to terror. But the play, the new play, was a wonder, and I'm told that I accepted it for publication before a production was agreed. That play was *The Gigli Concert*. The previous one, *The J. Arthur McGuinness Story*, was properly buried.

I've always resisted the temptation, even the invitation, to speak of my editorial collaborations with authors. There's some kind of privacy to it, something akin to the omertà of the confessional. The editing of plays for publication differs, however, from the kind of hands-on editing with which I engage with poets on their collections. The kind of invisible mending to which we aspire is more often the work of a dramaturge, script editor or director. With plays that we issue on their opening nights, we work to incorporate any changes, cuts or rewrites that occur during rehearsals. But it happens, and this is especially true of Kilroy's work, that sometimes the texts we publish don't correspond exactly to the words spoken and heard on the stage, and that's simply because changes have been made due to the specifics of the production: an actor struggled to say a phrase or line, perhaps, or a director's whim didn't correspond with the text the author prefers.

I've long ago explained my comprehension of publishing, the kind of literary publishing to which I'm dedicated, as a way of praising, and a way of protecting and preserving. Plays can enjoy an afterlife in the memory of those sometimes few who have witnessed the magic of their productions, or as influences, but in printed texts they can be made available for generations of readers, directors, amateur companies and students. Access allows assessment. They can help avoid that continuing shock, in the circumstances of Thomas Kilroy's art, not that it is not published but that it's not regularly or sufficiently produced. There are plays of his that I've never seen, some I suspect which haven't been produced in Ireland in my adult life, and others which have yet to be revived. And that isn't right, but it is something that could be put right. Through published texts assessments of a playwright's work are possible. In them we will see that Thomas Kilroy endures and, yes, will prevail, as one who keeps shape, and re-shapes, and finds new shapes for our theatre. As much as he recognizes Ireland as an island his work rebuts its insularity and isolation. He is a bridge-builder, whose work has enlarged our theatre. It has been a privilege for thirty years and more to have been a part of that process, backstage, offstage, looking after, as Mrs Einstein is said to have said, the little things. And long may it be so.

6 | An Extract from the Play 'Blake'

Thomas Kilroy

Scene Two: Blake Is Interrogated

Daylight. Finchley Grange Private Lunatic Asylum, London. Upstage a gallery. This looks downstage into a white, empty room. The Asylum Proprietor, Dr Hibbel is in the gallery with his guests, Sir James and Lady Fetchcroft. Below them, in the white room, stands a solitary keeper.

Dr. Hibbel. (*To keeper below*) You! Be prepared to bring in the lunatics at my command.

Lady Fetchcroft. Now, this Blake, Dr. Hibbel? You speak of him as if he had some secret powers –

Dr. Hibbel. Powers, perhaps, Lady Fetchcroft, secret, no. I never admit the secret in my practice of lunacy. Get it out in the open, I say. Out! Out!

Sir James. For heavensake, man, when are we to have these lunatics exhibited before us? Must we wait all day?

Lady Fetchcroft. I must see this Blake. He is exactly the kind of specimen needed for my study of the insane. You know, there is an alarming increase of madness throughout England today.

Dr. Hibbel. Indeed, madam. I would go so far as to say that madness threatens the very security of the realm.

Sir James. Where have you been living these several years, Hibbel? We are still at war with that little tyrant Bonaparte. Our treasury is exhausted. The country is riddled with Luddites and Jacobins and societies for the betterment of this that and the other and you talk to me of lunatics!

Lady Fetchcroft. I see, Dr. Hibbel, that it was a mistake to have brought my husband with me –

Dr Hibbel. I fear you do not see lunacy in the eyes as I do, Sir James. Behind the eyes, churning, churning, everywhere.

Sir James. Fiddlesticks! Your lunatic is in the bottom of the barrel to be put away for the sake of hygiene –

Dr Hibbel. Madness is like a curtain. Once we draw it aside, no mean feat, may I say, we may then see where Reason has been damaged and a cure may begin.

Sir James. There is no cure, sir! Your madman is a defect in Nature to be put out of sight! This is why we build walls and erect doors.

Dr Hibbel. You are not interested in madness, Sir James, is that it?

Sir James. I am a police magistrate, sir. If you have one or two criminals in your charge, show them forth and I may perk up.

Dr Hibbel. But why, may I ask? Why, then did you request this audience of the lunatics?

Sir James. (*Explosion*) Why? Why – because of that woman there! (*Lady Fetchcroft*.)

Lady Fetchcroft. Pay no heed to him, Dr. Hibbel. He is on his hobby horse.

Sir James. She is not content to observe criminals in the Bridewell but now she must see lunatics in the asylum as well. She speaks lunacy to me at breakfast, dinner and supper and in between –

Lady Fetchcroft. I have studied lunacy in Dr. Monro's private asylum at Clapton. I have been conducted by the eminent Dr. Williams through the Collegium Insanorum at St. Alban's –

Sir James. What? I did not know this!

Lady Fetchcroft. I am a scientist, Dr Hibbel, such as yourself –

Sir James. Scientist! Hah!

Lady Fetchcroft. Yes, scientist, though you are incapable of knowing it!

Dr Hibbel. Please!

Lady Fetchcroft. (*To Sir James*) Return to the manor, husband. Don't worry, Dr Hibbel, his temper will soon abate once he has his gout in the ashes. I will remain and make note of Dr. Hibbel's work offering suggestions of correction when I think fit –

Sir James. No, madam! I haven't the slightest intention, madam, of leaving, so that you may indulge yourself in a lunatic asylum!

Dr Hibbel. Now-now!

Sir James. I am well aware of the antics you get up to in my absence.

Dr Hibbel. Very well (*Signalling to the keeper below*). Let us introduce the two lunatics.

Lady Fetchcroft. Two? A mere two? Male or female?

Dr Hibbel. One of each, Madame. Male and Female. My asylum is for the select few not the hordes, the paupers.

Lady Fetchcroft. We will see this fellow Blake?

Dr Hibbel. Yes, Lady Fetchcroft. But, first, an interesting female.

Sir James. Get on with it, man, get on with it!

The keeper leads in a beautiful young woman. Dressed in a white shift, she is oblivious of everything around her. All her attention is focused upon a tray in front of her which she carries on a sling around her neck. On the tray is a variety of small tools and machines which she constantly tinkers with. The sense is of a master machinist at work on small, intricate machines.

Dr Hibbel. Now, this young woman is of a most excellent family background but I am not at liberty to mention her name –

Lady Fetchcroft. What is her condition?

Dr Hibbel. Silence.

Sir James. You mean she's dumb?

Dr Hibbel. For seventeen years she lived a perfectly normal life within the bosom of her family. Her education, including several languages, was exemplary. Her health, according to several eminent physicians, was perfect. Then one day, she ceased to speak. She hasn't spoken since.

Sir James. Look at her hands. She is fiddling with something there. What is she fiddling with?

Dr Hibbel. Machines. She makes these minute, intricate devices –

Sir James. To what purpose?

Dr Hibbel. There seems to be no purpose to them. The devices seem to be mere toys with which she entertains herself.

Sir James. Good God!

Lady Fetchcroft. Is she a virgin?

Sir James. And that will explain all, I take it, madam? Whether she has been rifled or no? That's it, is it?

Lady Fetchcroft. My husband, Dr Hibbel, has no notion of the hysteric storms which the female is prone to. Nor what causes them.

Sir James. Stop! That's enough! Bring on your next lunatic, for Heaven's sake, man.

Dr Hibbel. Bring on Blake!

The silent woman remains behind, standing to one side, busy with her work before her on her tray. Blake is conducted on, still in the straitjacket. He is by now in a pitiable condition, frantic and moaning. At first he is unaware of anyone else.

Lady Fetchcroft. How do you describe his madness?

Dr Hibbel. He sees visions.

Lady Fetchcroft. Are these daylight dreams?

Dr Hibbel. Madam, he talks of moving across the known globe and out beyond the stars into the great void. Nor is time an obstacle to him as he shifts from ancient Jerusalem to our London before the clock strikes. He populates these great spaces in his head with figures of his own invention. He gives these figures outlandish names like Oothoon, Theotormon, Orc and Urizen. He calls them his giants and sometimes his fairies.

Sir James. That's all right then. The fellow doesn't even live in the present day. Anything else?

Dr Hibbel. I'm afraid you're mistaken, Sir James. He lives very much in the present day –

Sir James. Yes but rambling, surely?

Dr Hibbel. Rambling! Why he follows what is happening on our streets better than a newsheet. He is now much preoccupied with the war, the King's health and state of the nation.

Sir James. Oh, he is, is he? The King's health, eh? I must interrogate him, then. At once!

Suddenly, Blake and the silent woman become aware of one another and everything changes. He begins to circle her in a kind of awe, while she watches him intently.

Dr Hibbel. One moment, Sir James. Have you seen that? She responds! She has not recognized another presence in the house before this. (*To keeper*) Remove the waistcoat from Blake!

Lady Fetchcroft. (*As the keeper releases Blake*) Will he ravish her?

Dr Hibbel. There are times when I must throw the lunatics on one another to release what is hidden –

Blake. (*To the silent woman*) Speak to me! The Word! Whose Emanation are you? Do you come from the Great Eternity? You may tell me. I have already been there and back. You see, I was born once and have died many times since – Let me touch you – (*He touches her cheek.*)

Lady Fetchcroft. He is inflamed!

Sir James. Be quiet, woman and let the fellow damn himself in his own words.

Blake. Take me with you out of this vegetative world. We will walk together in Eternity and I will forgive you and you will forgive me. (*Anguished*) I'm unable to forgive, you see. It's as if I am frozen within or maybe consumed with a great fire. Jesus my Saviour tells me to forgive. How to forgive even he who would destroy you? (*Shift. Conversational*) Do you know the worst thing about this place? No? They do not allow me to work. No paper. No colours. No anvil for Los to hammer out thunder of thought and flame of fierce desire. (*Looks in her tray*) What have we here? Is this your work?

She becomes terrified, tries to break away from him, making inarticulate cries of fear but he pursues her, almost bullyingly.

Blake. Let me see! (*A device falls from the tray and she runs and cowers away from him. He lifts the object up, gingerly, to the light and* *explodes in a rage.*) A machine! This woman has given herself to the machine, the furnace, sword and smoking ruins! Wheels turning, cog on cog, molten metal flowing in channels through the female ovarium, soft wire drawn in lascivious delight from her bowels, body of Death in the female tabernacle – (*Throws the metal object*) Get out of my sight! (*She runs off.*)

Dr Hibbel. (*Calling out, from above*) She is innocent, Blake!

Blake. (*Not looking up*) Innocent! Innocent!

'Bind him down, sisters, bind him down and with a screw of iron, fasten this ear into the rock!'

Dr Hibbel. Call her back, Blake. She may speak to you!

Blake. There is no innocence among the mechanics and in the mills. There is no innocence where the loins of Urizen spew smoke of industry.

Sir James. A bloody Luddite, bigod –

Dr Hibbel. Urizen! Who is this Urizen that you constantly speak about, Blake?

Blake. (*Calming*) Aha! It is my doctor of mental surgery, sitting on high, is it not? You should know, dear doctor who Urizen is because you are one of his instruments with your chains and your locked doors.

Dr Hibbel. It is best for you, Blake, that you be restrained –

Blake. Who are you to say what is best for any man? The apostles of Urizen are Newton and Locke and Reynolds and all those who would stamp out the Divine Imagination.

Lady Fetchcroft. Which others would you include in your strange lists?

Blake. (*Sadly*) Ah, lady, all those who having no passions of their own, because no intellect, spend their lives curbing others by the arts of poverty, cruelty and war –

Sir James. Have a care, fellow, what you say! We <u>are</u> at war. At this moment our armies and navies seek to put down the tyrant Bonaparte in the name of civilization...

Blake. I make no distinction between Nelson, Pitt and Napoleon –

Sir James. Good God! This is not madness, this is sedition! Sedition!

Blake. Dr. Mad? Who are these two comical spectators up there beside you?

Dr Hibbel. Now-now, Blake! These are Sir James and Lady Fetchcroft, persons of authority –

Blake. Shite upon authority!

Sir James. Bring the fellow here before me. Now! This will have to serve as my bench.

Lady Fetchcroft. It is not a common madman. It is a kind of preacher.

Dr Hibbel. Oh, Blake, see where your mad visions have led you! Turn back from this road before it is too late –

Blake. (*Dreamily*) When I take my walk down the lane I can touch the sky with my stick.

Lady Fetchcroft. I can speak to him! I know I can!

Sir James. Shut up, woman. Drag the fellow before me. At once! (*The two keepers do so and Blake stands trial.*) Now, fellow. No beating about the bush, mind! What are your politics?

Blake. I'm a republican because of the shape of my head –

Sir James. Hear that! Attend to it! This fellow does not belong in an asylum. He belongs in a penitentiary. A dose of solitary would do him good.

Dr Hibbel. No, no, Sir James, he is in my care.

Blake. (*Almost casually*) My wife has gone to hire a lawyer. I will be out of here before dinner-time.

(*Then, chanting loudly*)

>A fourfold vision is given to me;
>Tis fourfold in my supreme delight
>And threefold in soft Beulah's night
>And twofold Always. May God us keep
>From Single Vision and Newton's sleep –

Dr Hibbel. See, Sir James! Mad, absolutely mad.

Sir James. (*Uncertainly*) I will send my runners to take him before the Bench for proper arraignment and judgement.

Lady Fetchcroft. Oh, husband, where is your sense? He would make a mockery of your court of law.

Blake. 'Go, Noah, fetch the girdle of strong brass, heat it red hot,

Press it around the loins of this expanding cruelty –'

Dr Hibbel. Besides I have the papers, Sir James, sworn before two Justices of the Peace for his confinement –

Blake. 'Weep not so, sisters, weep not so –'

Dr Hibbel. You below! Remove the lunatic Blake immediately to his cell!

Blake. (*As the keepers seize him*) Lay off! I am here because I must pass through Evil and out the other side. I must feel it as if it rises from my bowels and touches my skin like the sting of leprosy. My guide is not the Yea-Nay-saying Creeping Jesus of the chapels who is friend of all mankind. No! My Jesus has the wrath of the tiger on his tongue and uses the rod and is in the wilderness. (*He stalks off, with dignity.*)

Lady Fetchcroft. Well!

There is a single, piercing female scream, off.

Sir James. What is that? (*The screaming as before but lower, more breathless*) What further gibbering display do you have for us, Hibbel?

Lady Fetchcroft. It is – a female –

Dr Hibbel. (*To a keeper who has returned*) What is that howling?

Keeper. It is the wife of the madman Blake.

Dr Hibbel. The wife! And where is she?

Keeper. She is roaring before the front gate. Will I turn her towards the highway, sir?

Dr Hibbel. No, no, admit her. It is the very trick I need. (*The keeper leaves.*)

Sir James. What will you do?

Dr Hibbel. It is often the way into a madman's mind, the path taken through someone close to him. Wife or child.

Lady Fetchcroft. But will she be used by you in this fashion?

Dr Hibbel. She is simple. She will not suspect what is happening. For I will have to break him in his obduracy as one would an unbroken colt. I will have to lift the curtain and see where Reason has withered within him. And then I may make him whole again. Or I may not.

A dishevelled Catherine staggers in with the keeper. She can hardly stand with the fatigue and her blistered feet.

Catherine. William! William! Where is William?

Lights down.

7 | Panel Discussion 1: Reading Kilroy

Chair: Christina Hunt Mahony
Adrian Frazier
Declan Hughes
José Lanters
Christopher Murray
Peter O'Rourke

Christina Hunt Mahony. On this panel our brief is largely to discuss the reading and the writing as opposed to the more performative aspects of the theatre. I have the distinction of being the only person on the panel who was a student of Thomas Kilroy, at UCD a very long time ago. One subject that has intrigued me is how Kilroy represents historical and biographical figures, in a way quite different from the generations of rather dead historical plays that everyone was used to. Adrian, I know that you have an interest in this.

Adrian Frazier. I was reading *The Big Chapel* just last week which I think holds up extraordinarily well – there's an abundance of talent already visible there. In the 2002 *Irish University Review* dedicated to Kilroy's work there is an article by W. Nial Osborough about the real and quite extraordinary incidents that took place in Kilroy's home town of Callan between 1867 and 1876 and inspired the novel.[1] Throughout his work, from that novel and the early plays right up to the present day, Kilroy has taken historical material and reinterpreted it creatively in an extraordinary variety of ways. He's not the first person to do this of course – in *Hail and Farewell* George Moore wrote what he called 'A novel with real people in it', and claimed to have quoted from real

---

[1] W. Nial Osborough, 'Another Country, Other Days: Revisiting Thomas Kilroy's *The Big Chapel*', *Irish University Review*, 32.1 (2002), 39-67.

conversations and encounters he had had with these people. But the characters were always representatives, appearing to Moore's own consciousness – he didn't go inside their consciousnesses. Joyce did something comparable in *Ulysses*, which has some real people in it. A.E. is in it, John Eglinton is in it, the library scene features a lot of real people, but again you see these people through Stephen or through Leopold or through Molly. You don't actually enter their individual consciousnesses.

In *The Big Chapel*, and of course in the plays, you see all of the characters from the inside, regardless of whether or not they are based on real people or not. Kilroy uses free indirect discourse to represent their thoughts and capture the voices with which they spoke when they were speaking to other people. It's like they're talking to themselves in many instances – he has a real ear for dialogue in that respect. Through this historical recovery you get a total interpretation of a figure about which you could only know a little from the outside.

I think that raises fascinating issues – I remember going to see Derek Mahon after a performance of *The Secret Fall of Constance Wilde* and he was hopping mad, saying it's terrible what happened in that play, you can't represent Constance Wilde's consciousness because she was a real person, and you can't make her say things she didn't say. The same goes for Oscar Wilde, for that matter, because these people own their own afterlives, so to speak. The basis of Kilroy's approach is that you use historical figures as if they were symbolic figures, and you make up things for them to do and say that they did not do and did not say.

When he wrote *The Big Chapel* and the plays this was a novel thing to do, but everyone is doing it now – look at Colm Tóibín's novel about Henry James, which has all kinds of non-Jamesian thoughts in it. I'm half-way through David Lodge's novel *A Man of Parts* which is about H.G Wells. The whole thing is incredibly well-informed but he also enters into the consciousnesses of all the figures, and is making all of that up. It's fascinating to be able to step into figures' minds in this way. Speaking as a biographer it's the one thing you are not allowed to do – you try and get the reader to make inferences about what's in the mind of the subject, but you can't make the inferences yourself.

Declan Hughes. When Rough Magic started we were about twenty-one or twenty-two, and we were down on many Irish writers. We thought we were a young generation with something new to say, but the first play we did was *Talbot's Box*, set in the early part of the twentieth century.² This tells you something about the relation between Kilroy's work and historical figures – it was an utterly modern play, which refracted a street art of early twentieth-century Dublin through a very modern consciousness. Matt Talbot is the irreducible core of the play, an isolated figure set against a carnival of other forces who want a piece of him. As an individual Talbot faces social pressures, religious pressures and cultural pressures, all of which are trying to violate his integrity. That tension between the individual and the forces that make demands upon him is one of the central energies of Kilroy's work.

That optimistic American sense of the individual as someone who is capable of withstanding that pressure and is capable of changing may be the key to why I've responded so strongly to his work. Many other Irish playwrights of his generation didn't see the light at the end of the tunnel, and felt that the social forces or the forces of faith were too heavy and too strong. Of course, the green light at the end of the shore is always illusory – it leads you on but you won't make it – but I think it's always there in Thomas Kilroy's work. Anyway this brings me to the time when Rough Magic did *Tea and Sex and Shakespeare* – we obviously knew Tom, but somehow we became known to him. He had done the play at the Abbey in 1976, and I can't remember if we contacted him or he contacted us, but it became clear that he wasn't entirely satisfied with the text of that play as it had been produced. We just jumped at the opportunity to work with him on anything really and so we came together.³ *Tea and Sex and Shakespeare* is a surreal farce, but there's something very dark at the heart of the play, and talking with Tom in the early stages we discussed what this was. The problem with a writer when he's blocked is that he can't distinguish the art from the life. Brien, the playwright who's at the centre of the play, can't distinguish what is a subject for drama from what isn't. So everything in life becomes material and consequently nothing is material. It's a kind of madness, a continual sequence of category errors as the scientists say. And that is his condition. Underlying this there's a kind of *Who's Afraid of Virginia Woolf?* scenario in the marriage. There's a child, there are continual references to suitcases, to hats, there's sexual fear, there's very Freudian symbolism of wombs and vaginas, Brien's afraid his wife is cheating on him. Gradually we come to the understanding that there has been a miscarriage, or a stillbirth, an abortion, something that scars the marriage. Reading it again I realized – I think I'm right in

---

² *Talbot's Box* was presented by Rough Magic at the Players' Theatre, Dublin, in 1984.
³ *Tea and Sex and Shakespeare* was presented by Rough Magic in a number of venues around Ireland and finally at the Project Theatre, Dublin, in 1988.

saying this – that the only line that actually takes place in reality is the very last line, when his wife comes home from work and says, 'And how was *your* day?'

Before then we've had scenes where his wife has come out of the wardrobe, where the next door neighbour Sylvester has appeared with all these suitcases, or with a huge pair of castrating scissors. The middle class mother and father-in-law appear at one point. Everything is hyped to the status of a nightmare. I think the original version of the play had more of a binary structure: it was a naturalistic play into which the surrealistic, the nightmarish, the dreamlike elements arrived. Luis Buñuel came up a lot when we were discussing the play, and we had the sense that maybe these things don't always need to be logically explained. Gradually the play moved further towards becoming this kind of infernal machine – it is a surreal farce, and a farce that is quite brutal.

Christopher Murray. Following Declan's remarks, in the first place I would wish to argue that Kilroy's imagination is consistently dualistic. You may recall Richard Kearney's attempt some years ago in his book with that title to define 'the Irish mind'. Kearney contrasted the Irish sensibility with the empiric British mind, where truth is amenable to description, definition, and proof in quasi-scientific terms. He argued that the philosophical procedure in establishing truth along British lines could be summarized as 'either/or', that is, one could arrive at a choice in which fact triumphs over what is demonstrably non-fact, an alternative to be discriminated without ambiguity. The Irish mode of thinking, on the other hand, Kearney described as 'both/and', a recognition that truth is ambivalent when both sides are given due weight.[4] So far as Irish artists are concerned this account of the Irish mind is, it seems to me, valid because it takes into account the dissenting nature of the Irish character and of the Irish imagination. What was it Berkeley said? 'We Irish see things otherwise'? Something like that. Andrew Carpenter has written of the 'double focus' in Anglo-Irish literature (as the preferred term then was in 1976) from Swift on through Synge and, I daresay, Beckett.[5] I would include Thomas Kilroy in this argument. Par excellence, his art is characterized by 'double vision'.

---

[4] Richard Kearney, 'Introduction', in Richard Kearney (ed.), *The Irish Mind* (Dublin: Wolfhound Press, 1985), pp. 7-38.
[5] Andrew Carpenter, 'Double Vision in Anglo-Irish Literature', in Andrew Carpenter (ed.), *Place, Personality and the Irish Writer* (Gerrard's Cross, Bucks.: Colin Smythe, 1977), pp. 173-89.

Further, in contrast to Friel or Murphy, Kilroy does not present linear narrative but rather a story which divides against itself or which focuses on a character at war with him or herself. There is always a folding over or a doubling back in the process, and the art lies in finding the theatrical means to make this conflict both clear and explosive for the audience. Two quick examples: *Double Cross* and the recent radio play *In the Garden of the Asylum*, where Kilroy brings into the same space two distinct narratives which did not and could not happen in life or nature but which are so artfully juxtaposed and developed that a credible interaction and newly born drama results.[6] This happens through the medium of performance chosen. In *Double Cross* the same actor plays William Joyce and Brendan Bracken; in the radio play the medium of radio allows the sharing of space by Lucia Joyce and Bosie's son. The impossible, the factually contradictory, is rendered possible by imaginative daring. This daring defines Kilroy's individual talent.

A similar interest in duality is seen in Kilroy's intense interest in form itself. Several of the plays have as protagonist an artist or visionary. This focus allows a concentration on form as a projection of the mind or consciousness of the artists, although care is taken always that this does not become bloodless. Thus *Tea and Sex and Shakespeare* features a writer wrestling with writer's block while his marriage disintegrates and his surroundings seem to close in on him: here expressionist use of space serves the theme wonderfully well, when combined as it is with comedy derived from native sources, O'Casey and Denis Johnston in particular. In *Talbot's Box* we see Kilroy's supreme ability to write 'outside the box', if you'll excuse the pun. In writing about social claustrophobia, incarceration of the individual consciousness, Kilroy actually opens up the black box, the modern theatrical space, so that it takes on epic as well as mystical considerations. Within the main action, the mysticism of Matt Talbot is at war with the world, the flesh and the devil and this psychomachia is reflected in the scenic design for the play and the cross-gendering of certain key roles, whereby shock and enlightenment conflict and provide growth in audience awareness. So in a Kilroy play the idea of form is self-consciously present if not foregrounded. The audience is invited to share in the very process of creativity itself. Every play is a play-within-a-play.

---

[6] *In the Garden of the Asylum* was broadcast by RTÉ Radio One on 1 May 2011. It is available online at http://www.rte.ie/drama/radio/genres-history-inthegardenoftheasylum.html.

In his latest play, 'Blake', Kilroy is at liberty – as in *The Shape of Metal* – to have the artist voice his idea of creativity. But we should note how once again there is a folding over between the central figure and his fate, which is the plot of the play. Therefore, when we hear Blake articulating his ideas on how sketching is done we hear at the same time an ironic description of his own containment. For example, as he is drawing the Catatonic, Blake praises the use of line as he works: 'The more distinct, sharp and wiry the bounding line, the more perfect the art,' he says. And he goes on: 'Corruption comes with the wriggling line, the soft edge, the fuzzy distinction between this and that'. This use of the line depends on freedom, the main theme of the play. And the opponent of Blake's vision is the Enlightenment figure of the Doctor, who wants to break Blake and restore him – as the doctor sees it – to sanity. The Doctor justifies his brutal approach thus: 'That which resists understanding has to be hunted down and brought into control. Otherwise there is chaos!' He needs to restore 'the Blake who thinks in straight lines'. This conflict between artist and authority recalls Beckett's first novel *Murphy*, and I think a lot of Beckett may be found in Kilroy's work in general, in the sense that every Beckett play is a play about playing, in a world where some malign authority controls the script.

José Lanters. I think that the figures of the artist and the visionary and their predicaments are repeated in different iterations in the various plays. You can see it in *Tea and Sex and Shakespeare* – in a sense the predicament of the artist is simplified as well as complicated by the fact that Brien, the playwright, is in crisis because he can't write. But his relationship with his wife is also in crisis because he can't have sex with her, because if he has sex he can't write. But if he writes, if he focuses on his art, then he can't have sex with his wife. That is his predicament, he can't do anything because he doesn't know where to turn. And that leads to the psychedelic moments in the play.

In the course of the play Brien is really in pursuit of finding an inner secret, that inner core in the suitcase. I would see Sylvester, his neighbour who keeps barging through his door and depositing all these suitcases in the room, as Brien's shadow self perhaps, who keeps confronting him with what he hasn't confronted within himself. So it is only when Brien finally opens the suitcase and sees what is in there that he seems to be getting to the point when he can begin to write – but as soon as he sits down and starts typing his wife arrives home, seductively drapes herself across his desk, and says 'And how was *your* day?' That of course interrupts his writing once again. Brien looks out into the audience and knowingly winks, as if to say, you understand my predicament – in a sense he is back to square one, except that now he can stand outside himself and observe himself ironically.

The predicament of the artist who is torn between the self-exploration needed to achieve his vision and the demands of the family and the outside world is something that we also see in *The Secret Fall of Constance Wilde*, where Oscar Wilde has a vision of perfection that he wants to achieve in his art as well as in his life. He seeks the figure of the Androgyne, a perfect blend of male and female, in his relationships with both Constance and Bosie. We see the artist constantly struggling to get near to an impossible vision.

Christina Hunt Mahony. In 'Blake' we also see a fractious and fraught relationship between Blake and his wife Catherine, and in *The Shape of Metal* we see how the relationship between Nell the sculptor and her family has totally broken down. This tendency to rewrite versions of people and versions of history to show the artist in isolation – all of these states are difficult to convey, but if you resort to meta-theatrical tactics it becomes a bit easier doesn't it?

Peter O'Rourke. Absolutely – Kilroy has said in an interview with Mária Kurdi that the idea of writing historical fictions is paradoxical. He said on his writing about historical characters that he 'always tries to subvert factuality, because really, I have great difficulty in taking facts seriously'.[7] Of course, this is celebrated in 'Blake', in which Kilroy states at the start that the Blakes were never incarcerated in this fictitious asylum, and in his other history plays he plays greatly with the historical facts. In *The O'Neill*, for example, he sticks very much to Seán Ó Faoláin's biographical account of O'Neill, which claims that O'Neill studied in England and had a great deal of influence in the English Royal Court. There are now studies which argue that in fact O'Neill never studied in England at all: Hiram Morgan's book *Tyrone's Rebellion*, for example, elaborates on that.

But that just goes to show that historical 'facts' are always part of a performance – Kilroy gave the inaugural lecture at the opening of the Brian Friel Theatre in Belfast in 2009, in which he celebrated the work of Friel and said that seeing Hugh Leonard's *Stephen D* and Friel's *Philadelphia, Here I Come!* were real revolutionary moments, and really kick-started modern Irish theatre. What is key here – and he

---

[7] Mária Kurdi, '"The Whole Idea of Writing Historical Fictions is Paradoxical": Talk with Irish Playwright Thomas Kilroy', *Hungarian Journal of English and American Studies*, 8.1 (2002), 259-67 (p. 262).

really drew this word out in the lecture he gave in Belfast – is the fluidity of Friel's *Philadelphia*, which established a fluid space which had not been seen at the Abbey prior to that. Kilroy has taken on that fluidity, as you can see in *The Madame MacAdam Travelling Theatre* as well, where in addition to the travelling players, all the local inhabitants are performing identities, like Burke in his quasi-Nazi uniform.

Metatheatre is a way of making the audience realize that there are distinct lines between illusion and reality, as Chris was just pointing out there. As we said earlier, that last moment in *Tea and Sex and Shakespeare* where Brien lifts his eyebrow to the audience is the only line in reality in the play. But in fact even that is not real, because Brien is colluding with the audience, making them realize that everything they have seen is complete nonsense. This allows the audience to question the discourses that we are led to believe, whether these are historical discourses, about people like Constance and Oscar Wilde, Lord Alfred Douglas, O'Neill, Brendan Bracken and William Joyce, or religious discourses: in *Talbot's Box* we see a critique of the hegemony of the church. For me what we have to celebrate about Kilroy's oeuvre is that he really interrogates all of those hegemonic and totalizing discourses in our cultural and social life.

Christina Hunt Mahony. Let's consider some of Kilroy's adaptations of works by other playwrights. I think you'd like to start, Declan?

Declan Hughes. Yes, I think with *The Seagull* in particular there are two schools of Chekhov. There's the school that thinks that you can just do him in a reasonably clear translation, a theatreland play, where people wander around in linen suits and speak in Glenageary and South County Dublin accents. It all sounds like it's taking place in the green room of a theatre, and very often there's some sublime acting there, because they're taking a very reverent approach to Chekhov. It can work brilliantly – as in David Mamet's *Vanya on 42nd Street* which is actually set in a rehearsal room and is one of the most extraordinary versions of Chekhov that I know – but generally I just don't get it.

What Kilroy did with *The Seagull* was to transpose the play to nineteenth-century West of Ireland. I'm not sure you could do that with the following three plays by Chekhov, but *The Seagull* is in so many ways an impure play and a mixture of styles. It has that Chekhovian poignancy but it also has a lot of gossip, a lot of manners and a lot of stuff about nineteenth-century theatre and theatrical habits. So when you see it in a translated version that's set in Russia you're distanced by the translation but also by the fact that they are talking about nineteenth-century Russian theatre, until eventually the effect is overwhelmingly alienating.

By contrast in Kilroy's *Seagull* we see Constantine, this young Turk who believes in all this mystical stuff and who is really a forerunner of A.E. and W.B. Yeats. His mother Isobel, who is a star on the London stage, describes his play as 'Celtic rubbish' and 'Hibernian drivel', and the whole thing suddenly becomes extraordinarily powerful. To do a play in translation what you have to do is to enable it to take place – that's the first task for a writer, to figure out how the play can happen at all. Very often that question isn't even asked, let alone answered. I think in each of his adaptations, but mesmerizingly in *The Seagull*, this is the question that Tom asks and answers so satisfyingly.

Jumping back a little to *Talbot's Box* and *Tea and Sex and Shakespeare*, I just wanted to think about the rhythm of these plays. When we talk about theatre we often talk about the ideas. We talk about what the play is about and the form of the play because these are easier things to talk about, but rhythm is the thing, you know. Rhythm is in everything and rhythm is the physical experience of the plays. These two plays are not dissimilar – there's an individual at the centre and there's frantic activity all around them – rhythmically they seem to me like pieces of modern classical music, which very often follow a particular form, with jagged, angular phrases, and structures that coalesce and duel and fight with each other. You listen to this and it acts on you, but then suddenly the clouds part and this lyrical moment occurs. In *Talbot's Box* it's Matt Talbot's extraordinarily poetic language. In *Tea and Sex and Shakespeare* there are very brief moments with Brien's wife Elmina, where you can feel the pain of this marriage, you can feel that something is not quite right. And there's another extraordinary moment in that play where they play the dance scene completely straight. It's like a cartoon, or a great carnival has suddenly been torn asunder and the tragedy remains. But the music of these plays, the contrast between jagged music and great beauty is worth acknowledging, and I think it's something we often neglect.

Christopher Murray. Unlike so many of his contemporaries, Kilroy has not adapted any of the Greek classics. He stays with the moderns, from Chekhov to Wedekind and Pirandello. There is something going on here which deserves examination. Through his versions of such plays as *The Seagull*, *Ghosts* and *Spring Awakening*, Kilroy wants to find ways of once again expressing a 'double vision', of translating in such a way that a play about one culture becomes not just a play about another but also carries with it the original penumbra for the audience to complicate its perspective. There are no 'fuzzy lines' here. The audience is required to see each adaptation as a palimpsest, a practice of writing over other writing, so that an entirely new message is communicated. But an awareness of the exercise is expected and is part of the dynamic. No other contemporary Irish dramatist does this. Others who write adaptations or 'versions' usually retain the original form and characterization and simply point the audience in the direction of Irish connections by way of some Hibernicisms. Kilroy goes much further, finding freedom in the departures from the original setting, and at the same time underlining the degree to which his new characters experience tragic alienation from a social structure and cultural values which are literally foreign to them.

An analysis of *The Seagull* would reveal how the ingenious transfer to 1890s western Ireland opens up a two-way understanding of social and cultural crises. Nicholas Grene has already shown how *Christ Deliver Us!* dramatizes 1950s Irish issues while also delivering (in double focus) Wedekind's tragic vision. I want to spend a few moments here on Kilroy's version of *Ghosts*. The point I want to make concerns the use of time. Kilroy's version is updated to the 1980s and set 'on the outskirts of a small Irish provincial town'. The extraordinary achievement is, I think, that whereas the 1980s setting emphasizes certain implications of the original play for modern Irish society, it also goes beyond that topicality into prophecy. I have two examples of this. Firstly, the attitude towards the clergy. Oliver Aylward, the Oswald character, exposes the hypocrisy of parish priest Fr Manning's traditionalist view of modern sexuality, but Oliver's anger also has enormous contemporary resonance in this scene:

> **Oliver.** I'll give you despicable talk, immorality, the lot, the real thing, Father. And people you know well.
> **Fr Manning.** What people?
> **Oliver.** The ones who wine and dine the clergy, that's who. Our great businessmen and politicians. By God, when it all comes out, that'll be the day! All the dirty linen of the Faith of our Fathers![8]

Likewise the comments by the Mrs Alving character, Mrs Aylward, greatly sharpen Ibsen's feminism but also reach forward to what was at that time concealed beneath the surface of Ireland's social revolution. She says about 'ghosts', for example, that:

---

[8] Kilroy, *Ghosts*, p. 24.

Sometimes it's what we've been taught. Our minds are haunted by dead, ghostly teaching. The future will find it all ridiculous. They'll say: how on earth could civilized people believe in such rubbish? And meanwhile the place is full of haunted, suffering people. Specially women. Oh, yes. Always women.9

This latter emphasis is not in Ibsen's text. Mrs Aylward returns forcefully to the theme later on, beginning the passage with a hint of Clov's final great speech in *Endgame*:

They taught me how to be a good wife. They taught me how a woman should keep her place. A woman has the greater role to play in life, they said. Did you ever hear such rubbish? A woman has to lead men in the path of virtue, they said. Oh, how well they know how to control women! [...] Make them feel good and they'll do anything. Not any more, Oliver, I've learned my lesson.10

This feminist language struck a topical note in the 1980s, but it was written before Mary Robinson was elected President of Ireland and before women's voices were raised against the church and all the abuse of which it was to be found guilty.

I also want to come at the point of theatrical language in Kilroy's dramaturgy by extending briefly the examination of adaptations to his work on Pirandello. These two adaptations, of *Six Characters* and *Henry* (from *Enrico IV*), have not received sufficient attention, but they point up the degree to which Kilroy's imagination is suffused with theatricalism. For convenience, perhaps, we are on this occasion dividing the examination of Kilroy's work, as this panel considers the texts and the dramaturgy while a second panel will discuss the theatrical and production values. I would argue that for Kilroy this is actually a dangerous approach. The duality of imagination I spoke of earlier indicates that he is both a literary and a theatrical writer; it's not really feasible to distinguish one language from the other in his case.

Pirandello, as we all know, repeatedly asserts the interplay of theatre and real life, while interrogating what we mean by 'real'. Radically, he broke down the distinction as decisively as Shakespeare did in *Hamlet* and *The Tempest*, but to different effect. Kilroy builds on Pirandello's perceptions in order to re-affirm his own, which are less sceptical and more involved with exploration of acting as a form of truthful expression.

---

[9] ibid., p. 34.
[10] ibid., p. 56.

There is a moment in *Henry* which is more Kilroy than Pirandello, however, and it is worth considering since it shows once again how his imagination works. The Doctor, like the Doctor in 'Blake', is preoccupied with bringing what he regards as a madman back to sanity, and refers to the cliff-top scene in *King Lear* as justification of his technique in using shock to force Henry out of an assumed role as madman ('assumed' being an ironic and double-meaning epithet). You will recall that the scene in *King Lear* takes place between Edgar and his father Gloucester, supposedly at Dover Cliff, where Edgar conjures up the scene and Gloucester then leaps, as he thinks, off the cliff-top only to land on his face on stage. The scene continues as a lesson in belief, as Edgar persuades Gloucester that he has been preserved by a miracle. Kilroy takes over the scene as a lesson in pure theatre. His Doctor remarks in *Henry*:

> A single, shocking step across a void. Remember the old play? An old blind man is persuaded to step off a cliff, when in fact he is standing on a level floor. The human mind will accept anything my friend. Provided there is a key to unlock it.[11]

The Doctor, however, fails to see that the key lies in the imagination and in the artist's ability to use it. It is Henry the supposed madman who has this key, i.e. to create illusion. As he puts it, 'That's the mystery of acting. You can defeat the body'. To him all is theatre, the world as well as the playhouse: 'What a charade it all is! What theatre!' It is through performance, he argues, that we 'deal with our innermost illusions, our worst fears, our failures, everything that we have lost, our secret histories'.[12] The final phrase, 'our secret histories' lies at the core of all of Kilroy's own plays.

Theatricalism is part of the very language Kilroy uses for the stage. Obviously, plays such as *Double Cross* and *The Madame MacAdam Travelling Theatre* offer the clearest examples of this, but *The Secret Fall of Constance Wilde* isn't far behind. In these plays the 'secret histories' of the protagonists are revealed by means of artifice and illusion. By such means the duality of Kilroy's imagination discloses infinite riches in the theatre's small space.

José Lanters. *Christ Deliver Us!* is a play, as Kilroy himself puts it, *after* Wedekind's *Spring Awakening*, in time but also in the sense that it's not a straight translation or adaptation, but is his own play inspired by *Spring Awakening*. You might well think that an adaptation of

---

[11] Thomas Kilroy, *Pirandellos* (Oldcastle, Co Meath: Gallery Press, 2007), p. 119.
[12] ibid., p. 121, p. 125, p. 129.

Spring Awakening would work well in an Irish context – you have this play about young people growing up in a culture of sexual repression as a result of which horrible things happen, and you can see how that might recall Ireland of the 1950s. Wedekind's play is such an odd play, though – the subtitle of *Spring Awakening* is 'A Children's Tragedy', which of course refers to the horrible things that happened to those young people, but in some ways also suggests that the tragic elements of the play are somehow diminished.

Wedekind uses a strange carnival mixture of theatrical styles, including melodrama, comedy, farce and satire, and in some ways, even though tragic things do happen, the tone is sometimes quite facetious. This is perhaps due to the fact that the characters are motivated by a petit bourgeois ideal, where they are always trying to keep up with the Joneses, or trying not to let the side down. Because their motivations are quite petty, the tragedies that occur are diminished in some way. By contrast, when Thomas Kilroy is writing about Ireland in the 1950s (and of course we are still experiencing the fall-out of that time, in the form of the Ryan Report and the inquiries into the Magdalene Laundries and so on) he is dealing with subject matter that is still very much alive for so many people, and the tone of Wedekind's play would just be wrong for that.[13]

In many ways Kilroy's play is more serious than Wedekind's, but that also means there's a shift in the motivations of the characters. Consider Moritz in Wedekind's play, the boy who's not that clever, but whose parents are really pushing him so he's struggling in school. In *Spring Awakening* he ends up killing himself because he feels that he has let his parents down. It's tragic that he kills himself but at the same time it's a bit ridiculous – you can't take his motivation entirely seriously.

Then look at Mossy in *Christ Deliver Us!*: he is also struggling in school, but his father is a real tyrant, and some of his school masters are aware that his father is a violent man. Mossy goes through the trauma of going to confession and telling the priest about being interested in sex and so on, and the priest then betrays him by making him tell the

---

[13] The report by the Commission to Inquire into Child Abuse, chaired by Hon. Mr. Justice Sean Ryan, was published in May 2009; the report by the Inter-Departmental Committee to establish the facts of State involvement with the Magdalen Laundries, chaired by Senator Martin McAleese, was published in February 2013. See *Commission to Inquire into Child Abuse: Report* (5 vols.) (Dublin: Stationery Office, 2009); *Report of the Inter-Departmental Committee to establish the facts of State involvement with the Magdalen Laundries* (2013), http://www.justice.ie/en/JELR/Pages/MagdalenRpt2013.

same story that he's told in the confessional outside of the confessional. There's this betrayal within the school environment, and he's also facing the potential consequences of his father's violence: these factors ultimately lead him to kill himself. The motivation for that act is psychologically much more grounded and profound than in Wedekind's play, and I think throughout Kilroy's adaptation you sense a shift towards a much more serious undertone.

Christina Hunt Mahony. Now, I've heard a lot of people today saying they regret not having seen a particular past production of one of Kilroy's plays – I'd like to conclude by asking our contributors which play they would most like to see revived?

Adrian Frazier. I'd like to see *The Death and Resurrection of Mr. Roche*. I think it would come off as quite a contemporary play. If it had been sent into the Abbey five years ago I'm not sure they would have wanted to do it. They'd want something that reflected more politically correct ways of representing homosexuality. And the play was written before those were invented, basically. It's quite dreamy what's happening in that play. I think Peter Fallon said that he couldn't swallow it when he first saw it because he was sick to death of doing exams on Pinter, and there is something quite Pinteresque about it, there's a certain level of anger and malevolence about the characters that is still quite fresh.

Since we are an academic panel and since it's that time of year I think we should set ourselves an exam, with the question: what is the attitude to the individual in the work of Thomas Kilroy – discuss. You can imagine receiving with dismay three or four hundred essays, in which everybody said that the individual rebels against the institution of the church, and the freedom of the individual is celebrated, especially through the salvific figure of the artist. That would be the wrong answer, but everybody would give that answer.

Declan Hughes. You have to give us the right answer now, Adrian.

Adrian Frazier. Well, in *The Big Chapel* there's a scathing critique of Lannigan, the priest who rebels against the church and his bishop. He's not the hero of the book. There are heroic elements to his character but he is very profoundly criticized. Or look at Nell, the artist in *The Shape of Metal* – we see her daughter tearing her to pieces. Nell's still standing and still roaring, but only because she's an indestructible egotist. I think that often the artist figures in Kilroy's work have demonic elements that are enabling to them but destructive to others.

Individualism isn't so much celebrated as exposed to a question: if this is all we have, is this enough?

Christina Hunt Mahony. Now, Peter is of another generation and may have missed a number of these productions [*laughing*].

Peter O'Rourke. Indeed! I would most like to see *Tea and Sex and Shakespeare* because it sounds so chaotic, mad, and a wonderful farce, with all these characters coming in and out of walls and jumping out of windows, with suitcases appearing from here, there and everywhere, and with Elmina's complete *non sequiturs* that she's always throwing in, 'I am leaving for Australia!' and things like that. Kilroy said in an interview with Gerry Dukes some years ago – and Declan also alluded to this earlier – that one problem with the printed version of that play was that it stipulated a surreal setting, and that he wished in future editions to specify instead a naturalistic Dublin flat, 'as normal as possible'.[14] I think that the contrast that would arise between that kind of setting and the chaos on the stage would be very amusing.

In terms of the adaptations, which my fellow panelists have spoken about very eloquently, I think that what is striking within them is a great Kilroy-esque style. Like other Irish writers who have adapted the works of others, like Friel, Murphy, and Heaney, Kilroy's adaptations diverge significantly from the original plays. I think that's something to be celebrated but also reflects the way Kilroy has spoken about the theatre as a plastic art, echoing Tennessee Williams's idea of a plastic theatre. Kilroy has also said that the play is just a medium, that the writer is just a cog in a wheel; sometimes we can get very stuck on the separate roles of the writer, the director, the stage designer, and put these people in discrete boxes. Last night Nicholas Grene spoke about Kilroy's 1959 essay 'Groundwork for an Irish Theatre', in which he promotes the idea of a writers' theatre in which writers can workshop ideas and play around with things. The collaborative method, which is what Kilroy has passionately advocated throughout his career, results in the sort of drama which we are celebrating today, which is why I've alluded to his comment about changing the setting of *Tea and Sex and Shakespeare*: collaboration and playing around with ideas are essential to making this workshop theatre something tangible.

---

[14] 'Tom Kilroy in Conversation with Gerry Dukes', in *Theatre Talk: Voices of Irish Theatre Practitioners*, ed. by Lilian Chambers, Ger Fitzgibbon, Eamonn Jordan, (Dublin: Carysfort Press, 2001), pp. 240-51 (p. 244).

Christina Hunt Mahony. I think that play in particular would find a larger audience the next time round; it must have been hard work getting the audience on side when it was first put on. A newer generation of theatre-goers is used to a much more postmodern atmosphere in the theatre and would surely be more willing to go along with the imaginative structure.

Peter O'Rourke. Indeed. The postmodern condition is very evident in Kilroy's work and in every representation of a character or person in a Kilroy play you get this sense that there is no one definitive, true identity, and that we are always performing different things to different people.

Trinity College Dublin, 30 April 2011

8 | Panel Discussion 2: Directing Kilroy

Chair: Emer O'Kelly
Wayne Jordan
Marcela Lorca
Patrick Mason
Lynne Parker
Kevin Reynolds
Michael Scott

Emer O'Kelly. We are joined from the beginning by Wayne Jordan, Marcela Lorca, Lynne Parker, Kevin Reynolds and Michael Scott, all of whom have directed plays of Thomas Kilroy's; Patrick Mason is currently rehearsing tonight's reading of 'Blake'. Way back in 1959 Kilroy wrote of his excitement at the collaborative possibilities of theatre and of stage production.[1] A lot of writers aren't particularly concerned with these possibilities and concentrate solely on the text, so Kilroy is in many ways a director's dream, because he accepts that theatre is both performative and collaborative. He believes in what Umberto Eco has described as 'furnishing the room'. The novelist can furnish the room with detailed description, but with a play this must be done using the performances of the actors, the vision of the director and, literally, the stage set itself. That can be something as simple as three cubes, or it can be an extremely naturalistic set.

Wayne Jordan. *Christ Deliver Us!* was the first play I ever directed where the playwright was either in the country or alive.[2] So that was a big new thing for me. My work outside the Abbey had largely been versions of European plays or relatively new, formally inventive plays by English writers. During the time that I've been at the Abbey I guess

---

[1] Kilroy, 'Groundwork for an Irish Theatre', *Studies* (Summer 1959), 192-98.
[2] *Christ Deliver Us!* premiered at the Abbey Theatre, Dublin, in 2010.

I've been familiarizing myself with Irish drama and with Irishness. Irishness was never something I was very interested in myself; in fact I would say that when I was young I was embarrassed to be Irish. I remember the first play I saw in the theatre was a Shakespeare play – everyone talked in Irish accents and I was mortified by the whole experience.

So coming to do a play like this in Ireland was something I didn't really think I would ever find myself doing, or being involved in. I was incredibly taken by the text of *Christ Deliver Us!*. I was very excited first of all that *Spring Awakening*, which I had always loved, had been done in an Irish context.

What I loved about this play about adolescence and sexuality in Ireland was the way that it became a kind of bell jar into which we could look and investigate sex and what was going on at this moment in history with some distance. As a young gay man I was born into a world that seemed to me to have gone mad. There was no way of being natural, and my parents, who were absolutely wonderful, were very anxious about me and were constantly trying to force me into boxes and to be something I wasn't. School was very similar. The play raised some ghosts of things that had happened in my life, and I thought here's a great way to work with these issues and anxieties in a poetic way, and in a way that was about community and about history. The very Irishness of the play itself managed to reach part of the reason why I was embarrassed to be Irish.

Tom and I spent about a year talking through the play and text. I also spent some time in Callan. I was taken round and saw the workhouse, the big chapel and all the old places and went up to the old famine graveyard at Cherryfield. I went there with Fiach MacConghail, the Director of the Abbey and producer of the play, and we found sliotars all over the place which was really fun. I also went there with the set designer, Naomi Wilkinson. I felt I needed to know something about Tom's background, since *Christ Deliver Us!* recast this European classic in the world from which he had come.

Over the course of that time I discovered the existence of handball alleys, which I didn't know about and hadn't come across before. There are handball alleys all over Ireland and they are insane, brutal, concrete things that people used to go to and play handball in. Often they have just been left abandoned in the middle of fields, with weeds coming up through the concrete. I'm not too sure of the history, but I think that during the Civil War people used to have meetings in them. Of course, later teenagers would go there to have sex or to kiss or smoke marijuana.

The handball alley is a thing that was supposed to be there for us to play in and express ourselves but looks completely horrible – it really reminded me of the architecture of the school that I would have gone to, of the backs of churches, and of the schools I found in the rural parts of Ireland. I thought here was an image that reminded me of my childhood, cycling to the edge of the estate. I came from a suburb that was just on the edge of Dublin, and we'd cycle to the edge where concrete met grass. I guess for me the image of a big block of concrete on top of some grass gave a really strong sense of what the play itself was about, of oppression and weeds growing up through the floorboards.

I was also thinking about God, and where God is in the play. I don't believe in God; I used to and then one day it wasn't there anymore. When Tom and I were talking sometimes he would use the religious term absolution. I remember finding this very confusing, because I don't believe in absolution: it doesn't mean anything to me. But then slowly it dawned on me that Tom was reclaiming this language in a way, turning it round to make it something that opened up possibilities again. And in that moment I guess I suddenly realized something about myself and Irishness, and found a way that I could work in Ireland, in the Irish capital and on the national stage, which was a big deal for me personally.

Before that, like the young people in the play, I refused things that had come before me, but in that moment I guess I realized that the generations that came before fought hard and still were fighting. I felt part of something bigger than myself and I felt connected to that something, and in that moment I could suddenly see right through one hundred years of history, and see that there were lots of people like me out there trying really hard to get things done. I felt that was a good thing.

Emer O'Kelly. What Wayne may be saying is that we are slowly learning to absolve ourselves and to forgive ourselves. I think this leads us to Lynne Parker, who directed *The Shape of Metal* in 2003, a play about a woman who can't forgive her daughters and, effectively, can't forgive herself.[3] It's always fascinating when a writer in their more mature years decides to examine the nature of art as a topic. It's obviously extraordinarily revelatory; you find yourself in a privileged

---

[3] *The Shape of Metal* premiered at the Abbey Theatre, Dublin, in 2003.

voyeuristic situation where you can see how this writer who has fascinated you for so long has been able to produce their work.

Lynne Parker. It's always interesting when you are asked to talk about a play that you haven't directed recently. It's eight years since that production and it's been very useful and informative for me to look back on it and make some kind of an assessment myself of how the production had gone. It was a successful production – it did well, it was well received. But I want to do something a little unusual, and dissect some things that I think maybe I would do differently if I was to do it again. I think in retrospect that our production just missed something which I think I'm beginning to see now.

I want to talk a bit about the practicalities of the production. *The Shape of Metal* is a play with three people in it. It's essentially a conversation, and reading it again I was just awed by the brilliance, the spark, the flow, the purity of the writing. Contradiction is at the heart of any play, and this play has it in spades. The play takes the form of a conversation but this is increasingly intruded upon by memory. This makes it, as with all Kilroy's plays, playful.

When we were coming to do the piece there is one thing I think that proved quite problematic, but for the very best of reasons. The play was scheduled for the Abbey Theatre, which has a very big stage. There is no question that Kilroy is a major writer, and his work deserves to be produced on the main stage. There is an inbuilt challenge however, with a work of such density, where the drama takes place not only through the discourse but also through the behaviour of the characters – it's difficult to put this on such a huge canvas. The Abbey is an odd shaped theatre; the shape of the stage has curvature but not thrust, so from any one angle you are seeing a very similar version of the play. It's always one picture, and you have to construct a production like a picture.

The Shape of Metal is a play about sculpture, and what we ended up with was a piece that actually took the form almost of an icon. The character of Nell, played by Sara Kestelman in our production, is in her eighties and is almost immobile – if she had been placed at one side of the stage a lot of the audience would have missed what she says. Placing her in the centre of the stage created a kind of stained glass window effect, but this made it quite difficult to tap into the ley lines of the stage. Each stage has a dynamic underneath its surface, determining the movement and the energy of the piece. The Abbey has a very shallow stage, and its ley lines are tricky to negotiate. I would actually love to revisit that play and do it in the round with a big audience – I think then you would be able to see in three dimensions all the layers of contradictions within the play.

Nell is a fantastically, almost unseeingly subversive character, and uses language in a way which is dangerous, nasty and great fun. She's a wonderful creation: a conversation with Nell is like sliding down a cheese grater. Judith, the daughter who has to parry all of this, was played by Eleanor Methven. Eleanor is one of the most subversive people I know, and in some ways she was slightly emasculated by having to cope with this extraordinary character as played by Sara. One thing I think I missed and would really like to reinforce if I were to direct the play again is the fact that Judith is gay. In 1972, even in bohemian Anglo-Irish circles there's a dislocation from the establishment there. I think that we concentrated a little too much on the formality and strictness of Judith and just missed a ludic sense that, genetically, she must have – I think next time I would like to see that given a little more play.

That said, Judith is a person with whom you identify. Eleanor gave an extraordinarily sane and measured performance of this person who is in the middle of a recognizable enough situation: how do you cope with a genius? And that's a very interesting question for all of us now, at a time when we are looking at standards of behaviour and ethics and what is permissible. Judith is the one saying to her mother: you cannot behave in this inhuman way; you might be brilliant but it is inexcusable to be as damaging as you are. But of course, because it's a drama you get the inner story: you see the workings of Nell's mind and you see how troubled she is and that she allows herself no forgiveness. This is a fantastically three-dimensional piece.

I think one of the things that we did for the very best of reasons was to go for a naturalistic staging of the play. People have talked about how much theatrical mischief is written into Kilroy's work – the decision for a director is always whether to try and put that on the surface or to allow it to invade the production. We went for a naturalistic setting and I think we were probably right to do that, but it did give us problems. Staging the work of a great artist, a genius, you want to see evidence of that, which is really tricky to present – you are asking people who are prop makers and set designers suddenly to be great artists. And when they are great artists, there's always that question of who's to decide what a great piece of sculpture should look like. I think what we did was faithful but in a way it led the eye too easily away from the core, which was the conversation.

Time having moved on and theatre making having taken some very interesting new directions, next time I think I would concentrate more on what I describe as the liquid elements of production. That means lighting, possibly film-like projections; it means sound design, and the more spiritual elements of stagecraft, so that you could give suggestions of these things rather than the fact of them. I think that might refocus the play and give the audience space to imagine the work of art, which is always more powerful; the power of suggestion is our most effective tool in theatre making. I don't regret the decisions that led us to the original production, but the wonderful thing is that you can always come back to these. We are deploring the fact that Thomas Kilroy's work isn't performed more often and that's just down to the irritating practicalities of funding and what have you. But there is always the potential to return to the plays and rediscover them. I've got great grá now to come back to this particular piece and maybe solve some of the problems I didn't originally.

I also want to say that I think Kilroy's work is such a relief to read, as the work of someone who is not afraid to be articulate and to write eloquent English. So much of writing now is reduced to grunts, the inability to express oneself, and it's just like breathing fresh air again to read someone who not only allows his characters to use language to say what they mean, but to say more than that and push the boundaries of meaning.

Kevin Reynolds. I've worked as the series producer of RTÉ Radio Drama since 2003. At RTÉ we are privileged to produce and programme the very best of Irish dramatic writing. If there's been a dark note to this seminar this weekend it's been that people have missed certain productions of Kilroy's work, but I'm delighted to say that all our work at RTÉ Radio Drama, including *In the Garden of the Asylum*, which was commissioned for Tom's seventy-fifth birthday and broadcast in 2009, is available on demand online.[4]

I'm going to talk briefly about the genesis of that work. While a student at UCD in the 1950s Tom had read a book called *The Principles of Psychology* by William James. It was written in 1890, so it pre-dates Freud. James was the first to introduce the notion of streams of consciousness, which is so important to James Joyce's work. Kilroy's reading of this, along with his lifelong interest in the works of Joyce and indeed of Oscar Wilde, and, I would speculate, his reading of Carol Loeb Shloss's biography of Joyce's daughter Lucia which appeared in 2003,

---

[4] See http://www.rte.ie/drama/radio/genres-history-inthegardenoftheasylum.html.

were the seeds that germinated into *In the Garden of the Asylum*. The play dramatizes a fictional meeting between Lucia Joyce and Raymond Douglas, the son of Lord Alfred Douglas and grandson of the Marquess of Queensberry, who were both patients in a psychiatric hospital in Northamptonshire. There is also a parallel story going on in the play between Dr. Hermione Edwards and Dr. Bobby Davis, exploring the nature of psychology, the nature of care versus cure, and a variety of other things.

What first struck us in RTÉ was the beauty of the writing. We had never read anything that had been so wonderfully written between people who have, as they would say nowadays, special needs. And we began to look again at these lyrically beautiful, searingly emotional honest speeches, by characters who were supposedly out of their minds but yet knew their own minds, in contrast to the other inmates of the asylum who were indeed the doctors.

As producers our job was to foreground this basic paradox, and to explore the intellectual spine of the work, which was the honesty and the sincerity of Lucia and Raymond as it was set against the hierarchical agenda of obedience and compromise. These were themes that Kilroy had scraped at and left open, along with pre-Freudian and post-Freudian notions of the father/daughter/mother relationships and father/grandfather/son relationships of Lucia and Raymond respectively.

The dramaturg Jesper Bergmann and I travelled down to Galway to meet Tom, and we began to look at the structure of the play. As everyone has said Tom is an absolute gem to collaborate with – no matter who one is, one's tuppence is always taken on board, and he has a great respect for the fellow professionals with whom he works.

We discussed various elements of narration and dialogue. We began to wonder whether we should set out our stall at the beginning of the play, to tell the audience what the play was going to be about, or whether we should just jump in and let the audience work it out for themselves, which is more or less what we ended up doing. Then we moved on to the technical production, the choice of music, the acoustics and the location recordings – we recorded the play both in the RTÉ Radio Centre and out and about in the garden.

Thomas Kilroy is a writer who uses the prism of history to force us as an audience, and as directors, producers, and interpreters, to explore the mental landscapes that he creates. He forces us to look at the social and political reality of ourselves, of Ireland and of the Ireland in which he lives. I believe that in *In the Garden of the Asylum* he achieves this beautifully, and forces us all to examine our world and our reality, and as Lucia says at the end of the play, to question whether we are truly sane ourselves. Are we truly free?

Emer O'Kelly. I'd now like to introduce Marcela Lorca who has been Movement Director for the Guthrie Theater in Minneapolis since 1991 and is Head of Movement for the University of Minnesota/Guthrie Theater BFA Actor Training Program. She has worked across the United States and in 2008 she directed *The Secret Fall of Constance Wilde* at the Guthrie.

Marcela Lorca. I think someone said today that theatre is plastic, and when I think of directing Kilroy certainly that observation strikes me very strongly. He's an incredibly theatrical playwright: *The Secret Fall of Constance Wilde* was given to me by Joe Dowling, the artistic director of the Guthrie, because I had previously directed a production of Federico García Lorca's *Blood Wedding* that had a lot of surrealistic elements in it. I immediately fell in love with Kilroy's play and with the challenges that it posed. The play provoked a lot of questions: who are these puppeteers, why are they here and what is their function? The task of putting Oscar Wilde on stage was also daunting.

The play was an invitation for me and my collaborators and designers to ask a lot of questions about Victorian England, and also about contemporary America. In an effort to define the world of the play we decided to create a kind of empty space, a warehouse space where everything is possible, with a lot of found objects. It could evoke an attic, a heaven or a hell. We had these gigantic puppets, more like mannequins, that were stationed in different places and were like forgotten spirits in this space. Thomas Kilroy writes extensive stage directions which are incredibly provocative. I think I followed his stage directions pretty well in terms of timing, but in terms of the visual side of things I changed quite a lot.

I decided to sacrifice two of the six puppeteers and bring two musicians, a pianist and a cellist, into the fold. So we had puppeteers who moved the play, moved the characters and moved the puppets, but also sang this beautiful choral music accompanied by live musicians – I researched the kind of music Oscar Wilde loved and used works by some of his favourite composers and by Samuel Barber, whose music I felt was very appropriate for the kind of world that we were creating.

When Bosie appeared as a sculpture, from the ground up, a beautiful Bach aria was performed – it was very important for me to seduce the audience into accepting this world, into accepting this change of realities we've been talking about, and to lead them into the minds of the characters, a subconscious world of scenes that were not happening in reality but were playing in their minds. We used a lot of movement and music in order to create a sense of beauty and of fluidity, to draw the audience into these different, internal worlds, to accept them as part of the texture of the story.

There were certainly controversial moments in the production – I'm thinking of when Oscar is in jail in a very feverish state and Jesus appears to him as a vision that travels towards him. Jesus turns out to be Bosie. The 'Hallelujah', this most beautiful religious music is being sung by the puppeteers. As Bosie arrives next to Oscar, he lifts him and kisses him on the mouth, so I knew that moment was going to create a huge reaction in the audience. And we did get some letters once the production had opened to which I was happy to respond. Moments like that were very provocative, so we had to lead the audience to accept them. There were a number of openly seductive scenes between Bosie and Oscar. I hadn't seen anything like that staged in the Guthrie, and felt I needed to help the audience accept this love affair and witness the beauty the characters shared. Wilde's love of beauty was an inspiration to me and to the designer, in terms of choosing costumes, music, textures and puppets.

Through the stage directions, Kilroy obviously wanted the puppeteers to provoke the characters, to push them into facing their internal lives and the internal conflicts that were preventing them from being at peace. Constance's trauma is finally manifested on stage with a huge puppet of the father basically raping her in a stylized way. The puppeteers are constantly pushing the characters to go to places they don't want to revisit. I also felt it was very important that they supported the characters, took care of them, showed them tenderness and compassion as the writing unfolded. Although the puppeteers were silent, for me any character has equal weight if they are on stage, and the puppeteers are on stage from beginning to end. Their presence was hugely important to me, their ability to listen, to empathize, to be provocative or violent, was crucial to the rhythm and impact of the play.

Emer O'Kelly. Now we come to Michael Scott of the SFX City Theatre in Dublin, who directed Tom's version of *Ghosts* in 1989.[5]

Michael Scott. It's twenty-two years since we did the show – at the time HIV was a 'hot topic' and a killer. It just wiped everybody out,

---

[5] *Ghosts* premiered at the Peacock Theatre, Dublin, in 1989.

there was no hope at all. Now today however, you can meet people with HIV who are old, but in those days it was an absolute killer. And a subject not easily or often handled in the theatre.

Two years previously, in 1987, I had fought to bring *The Normal Heart* to Ireland. Literally fought. We tried to get funding, but we couldn't even get the Blood Transfusion Board to take an ad in the programme. Nobody would deal with us, nobody would deal in the media with HIV or Aids: it was taboo and in fact in Ireland, nobody officially knew anything about HIV or Aids at all. A year later in 1988, Tom came to Phyllis Ryan, who was an old friend and collaborator of mine, and a legendary theatre producer in Ireland, with the script of *Ghosts*. Phyllis said to me: I want you to do this play, you have to do this. I was director of the Dublin Theatre Festival at the time, and I said, cool, let's look at it. So Tom and Phyllis and I ended up having a series of meetings over a year as Tom rewrote some of the script and came up with some other ideas.

The diversity of Kilroy's work is very exciting. For each play, for each idea that he's written, he's almost assumed a different theatrical language, and it's his ability to shift through these things that makes them so extraordinarily exciting. He's not just a 'writer', he is a debater, and he debates in each of his plays the very nature of 'being', and you never know what he is going to do next. He's always going to surprise you.

In *Ghosts* his attention to detail, his attention to language, his attention to the power of the word and how it functions in the sentence, and to the place of the word in the sentence and the way in which it functions for the actor, is extraordinary. Christopher Nolan's *Under the Eye of the Clock* had been published in 1987 and I had just created a stage version of it with him, so I was highly sensitized at this time to the use of a word, how it worked, how many words were in a sentence, how a word worked in a sentence on its own, how when you put it with the other words it became a tune, and how a paragraph became a symphony. I remember working through the script with Tom and initially looking at it thinking that this was very simple, ordinary language, but in the hands of the actors we had it took on this dynamic power that just blew the audience away completely.

It was wonderful working with the actors in *Ghosts*, they loved the text. They trusted it, and when you have actors like David Kelly and Doreen Hepburn who trust a text you are off and racing with champion racehorses from the start. Rehearsals for *Ghosts* were hilarious. Most of the directing was done at tea breaks. That's when we'd sit and talk, we had a whole week of just talking about the play, and at tea breaks David would tell stories about the old days. And then they'd get up on the stage and these tea breaks would suddenly turn into extraordinary moments of theatre in the rehearsal room. Doreen's death is a serious loss to the theatre.[6] I remember at one point she wanted to change a word in the play. I'm ruthless: when I work with an author and we agree on the script, I will fight for every comma for the author every time. Doreen came up with this theory one afternoon that she wanted to change something – it was something simple – but I remember ringing Tom anyway. I think we had a conversation for about two hours about whether Doreen would change it or not. And Tom eventually reluctantly said, yes let her change it, go on. Next day she wanted it back! I said okay, how do I ring him and tell him you want it back? But that was it with Doreen, when you're working with someone like her, and you are working with somebody like Tom, these things are important, because the text is so precise, every word is measured.

When I'm directing a show I collect huge numbers of images, paste them into books and talk to the actors about them. For *Ghosts* we came up with the idea of a set that was a corner – reflecting the idea that the whole play was about people who were in a corner. We had a corner made which had a door, and another door which led into a greenhouse which was full of light, from which there was no escape – it was in that greenhouse that Oswald [Oliver] told his mother he had HIV in Part Two. The place was full of light at the end of the play. Every door in the room was closed, the shutters were closed but through the greenhouse you could see dawn breaking on the burnt down orphanage and this light bursting within, and Mrs Alving [Aylward] sat on the sofa, holding her son in her arms as if he were a baby again, who was effectively having an 'HIV fit' and the beginnings of pneumonia, with a bottle of pills, wondering was she actually going to have to bring about a euthanasia. Because at that time, the idea of HIV was a death sentence. Oswald [Oliver] was saying, [*paraphrases*] 'Take me out of my misery, take me out of this', and Mrs Alving's [Aylward's] dilemma was magnified even more than in the original. That was the interesting thing: Tom took the Ibsen play and modified it and expanded it and brought it into the twentieth century in a way that was shocking and violent and vibrant, and made us question who we were. None of us left the theatre feeling the same as when we had gone in: the play shook us all, and caused a debate about 'who we are'.

---

[6] Doreen Hepburn died in 1997; David Kelly died in 2012.

With Mrs Alving [Aylward] sitting there in her drawing room, debating with a Catholic priest with whom she had an longstanding affair – and Catholic priests remember are supposed to be celibate – Kilroy was also dealing with a whole series of things about the Church, about who we are as people and what we are hiding – and *Ghosts* is about hiding. Taken together, his linguistic, emotional and thematic investigations constitute an investigation of Ireland at the end of the twentieth century.

The size of the Peacock made you feel that you were part of this living room, as though the actors were almost coming off the stage and into the auditorium. The detail of the set was hyper-realistic, so that even the light switch more or less worked – I knew people who lived in houses like this. We were very specific about the knives and forks, the furniture, everything. The set was very spare but very detailed – we wanted to make sure that the detail of the language was reflected in the detail of the production. Kilroy's plays shake you – as I said before, you're not the same when you leave the theatre as when you came in. Why? Because he has characters you recognize, people you relate to, there are ideals in the plays that you find in your own life – these things rattle you, disturb, make you think and draw you into this journey with Tom, into the places that he wants to go to.

Often a playwright writes in a certain way, and you go into the theatre thinking: oh, it's going to be another exciting treatment of that particular play in this particular playwright's style, but Kilroy doesn't allow you to do that. Tom shakes the fuck out of you every time he writes a play, and challenges you and you have to think: oh, am I up to that one, okay I think I'll take that on…

Emer O'Kelly. And now Patrick Mason, who has just walked in from a rehearsal of 'Blake'.

Patrick Mason. I just caught the end of Michael's talk there and I think that his point that no two Kilroy plays are the same, that their theatrical landscapes are distinct, their demands are distinct and their disciplines are distinct, is very important. 'Blake' is no exception, and it has been very interesting, even within the austere confines of a rehearsed reading, to find effective ways of responding to these demands.

The play poses quite severe demands on the whole means of theatrical representation. It visits at a very deep level a relationship between word and image, as you'd expect I suppose from a play about William Blake. Word and image are two polarities in the play, between which flows the energy of imagination. And at the fringes of that particular imagination is madness. One of the central metaphors of the play is the madhouse, the eighteenth-century madhouse where the inmates were exhibited to wealthy patrons and visitors as a form of theatre. So there is a play within a play going on at the same time as everything else is going on. One of the great challenges of all Kilroy's plays is posed by the extraordinary layers within them, the way in which the intellectual landscape, the emotional and psychological landscape and the physical and visual aspects of that landscape are all combined to form these sorts of intense networks of theatrical energy. It is pure theatrical energy – I remember Kilroy saying to me once about writing for the theatre: 'You know, if it could be done any other way it isn't theatre.' I think that's the challenge that he makes to us all as theatre makers. He has this extraordinary instinct for that which is essentially theatrical, and he knows that if you can do it in any other form then in some way you are not doing it. I suppose he remains one of the most challenging playwrights in the Irish canon to work with because he is working on all of those levels.

Another aspect of Kilroy's work which has been particularly important for me is his role as a mentor. He is the most wonderful teacher and mentor, and over the past thirty-five years I've been very fortunate in having such a mentor as well as such a hard taskmaster. His patience, his generosity of spirit and his unrelenting critique of his work and your work is really extraordinary. I think that this is perhaps a hidden but huge contribution to modern Irish theatre, for directors, actors and for fellow playwrights. In the best sense of the word there is something monastic about Tom's presence. He is a great mentor but he is also a great spiritual guide.

Trinity College Dublin, 30 April 2011

9 | Thomas Kilroy in Conversation with Adrian Frazier

Adrian Frazier. Thank you all for coming. Tom, could we begin where you began in Callan, and could you paint us a picture of life there, what it was like? Where were you with the family? What did your father do?

Thomas Kilroy. I think one of the interesting things about my generation is that we're the last generation to experience the foundation of the State, the War of Independence and the Civil War through memory, not history, through the memories of our parents and the stories that they told us as we were growing up. My mother and father came from the village of Caltra just outside of Ballinasloe, which is one reason I'm living in the West of Ireland. They were both involved in the War of Independence. He was an officer in the IRA, and she was a member of Cumann na mBan. So we grew up hearing stories of that extraordinary period. History sometimes enlarges events, whereas memory always brings it back to a human scale.

AF. And your father was in the Guards later on?

TK. Like a lot of IRA men of the day, he joined the unarmed police force. He was made a Sergeant, largely because they had no Sergeants. I think they were all made Sergeants in the beginning. I used to joke with McGahern about this. But my father was virtually confined to Callan all his life. He wasn't moved anywhere else, which was unusual, so we grew up in Callan.

AF. In the opening paragraphs of *The Big Chapel* you write that 'energy died in the place like a light going out and the town relapsed into timelessness. Time began to pass without much significance one way or another'.[1] Was it a place outside of time, the world you grew up in during the 1940s and 50s?

TK. Well, it was a war-time town; we had our Emergency. And as a youngster the town was shadowed by war. We didn't experience it as war, but it was there as a presence. I remember that on the main street in Callan there was lettering on the top of the building: 'Callan Town Hall'. And this was covered with canvas throughout the duration of the war. We were told that this was to divert any bombers that were passing overhead, and to make sure that they did not know that they were over Callan. Oddly enough the canvas stayed for years afterwards. Nobody remembered to take it down. But I do remember it as a place that had an almost cashless economy. I actually don't know how the mothers managed the weekly food rations. There were ten of us in our family, a typical Irish Catholic family. I went back there recently to visit the house with my daughter, and she was extremely shocked that ten children grew up in this small, terraced house in Callan.

AF. In 2010 *Christ Deliver Us!* caused a lot of articles to be written in the newspapers. And not too long ago you gave an interview about your schooling, and said that you didn't remember much criminal behaviour from the time, but that there was a lot of violence, or at least the sense of threat in the school. Did I get that right?

TK. Yes, absolutely. I never experienced any kind of sexual abuse in the school, but I think physical abuse in those days was something which was condoned. It certainly marked us. I think you experience that undercurrent of physical violence in Irish life generally. And I think it goes back to schooling. The school is St Kieran's College in Kilkenny, a great hurling nursery. I was back there recently giving out prizes, and they reminded me in public, to my shame, that I captained one of the few St Kieran's teams that lost a Leinster Championship. But you had to hurl, you know, there was no question that you didn't, you wouldn't survive if you weren't able to hurl. It was physically a violent place, but having said that it was also a school where you had six years of Latin and Greek. And that was an inestimable foundation for all kinds of things in the future, not least of which, writing.

AF. And would many of the lads from St Kieran's have gone on to UCD or university somewhere?

---

[1] Thomas Kilroy, *The Big Chapel* (London: Faber and Faber, 1971), p. 1.

TK. No, not very many. I mean, my mother and father left school at national school, which was typical of those days, but they were extremely bright people. And they had an obsession, both of them, with education. So how they did it was a bit of a mystery, but they managed to educate all ten of us, and a lot of us went on to third-level education. You had to win scholarships, of course, to do it, but it was the drive of the parents to make sure that you were going to be educated. They had this passion about education which I think was typical of their generation. I would say not too many would have gone on from St Kieran's. It was a diocesan seminary, and of course one of the functions of a diocesan seminary was to create young priests – the school itself was divided into a lay school and an ecclesiastical side. And the ecclesiastical side trained young men for the priesthood, mostly for the missions, as they were called in those days. You were expected to at least consider seriously the question of the priesthood, and you were surrounded by the Catholic system in full flower. A lot of my fellow Leaving Cert class would have gone on to the priesthood. If not to St Kieran's, they'd have gone to Maynooth and places like that.

AF. Humanism is a strong element in your work, in the sense of an individual trying to maintain dignity in the face of huge institutional structures. But at some point, if you're growing up in a very Catholic institution like that – UCD was a fairly Catholic place at the time too – did you have a sense that you were taking a different path or that your view of life was different from that of others?

TK. I certainly came up to Dublin in the early 1950s to UCD as a very gauche, insecure and inhibited young man. My brain was reasonably developed but everything else was dormant. The experience of Dublin and of the university obviously helped me develop, but I think it wasn't until I wrote *The Death and Resurrection of Mr. Roche* that I finally began to emerge out from underneath the soutane. I questioned the culture that I had lived with as a child in that play. It's a play which also, I think, addressed the destructiveness of people and the creation of homophobia. The writing of that play, I think, released me in a certain fashion. It was a very difficult play to write. It was based upon an actual incident which I had been told, a story I had heard in Dublin of an attack upon a female prostitute in a flat. As my archive will show, I spent a long time trying to write that particular play, and I couldn't get anywhere. And then one of those mysterious things happened where the imagination gives you a gift – I changed the female prostitute to a gay man, and the play wrote itself in a couple of weeks. My dear friend

Frank McGuinness says that this is not a play about homosexuality, and indeed it's not – the homosexual is the old traditional device to agitate the plot in the play. I knew very little about homosexuality when I wrote the play, so I think there is a kind of an unreal quality to the Mr Roche figure as a result of this. But in writing the play I think I threw off a few shackles.

AF. Ernest Blythe has taken a fair bit of stick over the years for rejecting that play, or for getting Tomás Mac Anna to reject it, but imagine the response if you sent it into the Abbey today. This is a play about killing a gay man: it's shocking, and still very cutting edge.

TK. Yes. I had two plays doing the rounds, that and *The O'Neill*. Maybe because I had the two plays doing the rounds neither of them was picked up. It took quite a while to get *Mr. Roche* accepted. Eventually a friend of mine gave it to Jim Fitzgerald, who was then a leading director in Dublin theatre. And he took it on, and then very quickly Niall Tóibín said he'd play in it, and Brendan Smith in the Dublin Theatre Festival backed it, so it happened in that way in the Olympia. But it was quite a while going grey at the edges before it found its home. And then as a result of that *The O'Neill* was accepted in the Abbey. But *The O'Neill* was written first. In fact the first thing I ever wrote in a dramatic form was a radio play. I had just started teaching at UCD at the time, and I submitted it to a competition run by the BBC in Belfast, and it won first prize. And that was my start with actors. I had a great cast: Cyril Cusack and Godfrey Quigley in the lead parts. It was, again, a play based upon an incident with my father. In those days the Guards were responsible for bringing mentally ill patients to the asylum. And my father came back one evening and showed us his finger, and his finger was completely white and damaged. Some misfortunate man that he was bringing into the asylum gripped his finger, and gripped it in the car to such an extent that all the blood went out of the finger. So that was the basis of my first play, the radio play, which was called *The Door* and was about this mentally ill man, and trying to get him out of the room and off to the asylum. And there was a Sergeant in that play, which was based upon my father, and there is the same incident – the gripping of the finger, which seemed to me a very powerful image.

AF. So by the late 1960s you were working at UCD, you had two plays written and a radio play, but you were also writing *The Big Chapel*. That novel had a great reception: it won several prizes and it was nominated for the 1971 Booker Prize. Did you think that this was the path you would take? It's quite strange that somebody writes a novel, their first novel, which is such a big hit, and that they don't go on writing novels thereafter.

TK. Well, I tried to write another novel, and it didn't work out. Oddly enough, now I'm writing fiction again. I'm writing a memoir, but it's a complete ragbag of a book. It started out as a memoir – I had cataract operations, and one of the effects of this operation was that I began to see very vivid memories, particularly of my mother and father and that kitchen in Callan. And things came back to me which I had completely forgotten about. So I started to write the memoir, but then I realized that I was writing something else – that I was writing a portrait of this town in County Kilkenny, and in order to write the portrait of the town I had to write some fiction. So I've written a fictional reconstruction, for example, of the Siege of Callan by Cromwell. Over the back wall of our house in Callan was a piece of ground called the Fairgreen, and up at the top of the Fairgreen there used to be a grassy mound, and as I grew up it was known as Cromwell's moat. The story in the town was that Cromwell placed his cannon on this moat, which was much bigger in those days, and bombarded the walls of the town at the other end of the Fairgreen. This fascinated me and so I've written a fictional account of the bombardment of Callan through the experience of two local boys. There was another incident during the Second World War which I'm also writing in fiction – just after the war we had an influx of German people coming to live and buy farms in Ireland, and I became fascinated by one couple who came to the area. The book may never be finished because it's getting very baggy and I have to find some kind of structure in it. I'm also writing mini-essays because I'm trying to explain to myself how I ended up the way I am after a lifetime, and trying to write about myself in relation to this extraordinary benighted country of ours.

AF. On the subject of writing in one form or another, it seems that the current crop of playwrights – people that are in their thirties – write as much for film as they do for the stage, or they go back and forth. But yourself and Brian Friel, your generation hasn't written as often for the screen. Is there some reason for that?

TK. You would have to ask Brian about his output. I do know that he shares with me a great love of film, and interest in film, and I think the same is true of Tom Murphy. I did write a couple of screenplays. The first one was a screenplay of *The Seagull*, which the BBC bought. Writing the screenplay is one thing, having it filmed is another—and it's a very tricky kind of business. In that case the BBC tied the film to a particular, big British star and she hemmed and hawed for several years and finally hemmed and hawed [*laughs*] her way off the project and as soon as she walked from it, it died. There was also an attempt to film *The Madame MacAdam Travelling Theatre* which was a Field Day play which never quite worked on stage, and Channel 4 decided that it could be made into a film. I worked for several years on that with a director called Declan Donnellan, a wonderful theatre director who wanted to film it. But overnight the film department of Channel 4 changed, and of course everything they had developed went with them. And that was the end of *The Madame MacAdam Travelling Theatre*. So I have written screenplays and I enjoy very much writing them. The great thing about screenplays is that you're paid even if they're never filmed. But I'd love to have a work filmed, yeah.

AF. How was it that you were drawn into working with Field Day? Could you talk about the aims of your participation?

TK. Well, I was the only director of Field Day from the South and the reason why I became involved was out of friendship. I was very friendly with Brian Friel, the two Seamuses, Heaney and Deane, and Stephen Rea, to the extent that before I became actually involved I was in a lot of discussion with them about what they were up to and what they wanted to achieve. At one point Deane asked me to write one of their pamphlets, and I was going to do that but instead Brian and Stephen came to my house in Mayo and asked me to write a play. I had just written a radio play on Brendan Bracken and I had this idea of doing a stage play using the two figures of Bracken and William Joyce, played by the same actor to create this doubling, mirror effect. I told Brian and Stephen about this plan and they encouraged me to go ahead, which I did, and then I joined the board. I knew something of the Northern situation before Field Day, largely from visiting Brian and going North with Seamus Deane. I was fascinated by the political potential of what was happening there, and in particular I was fascinated by the sectarianism, so it was a very natural thing for me to become part of the group in the end.

AF. I'm shifting gears a bit here, but you mentioned that Seamus Deane asked you to write a pamphlet, and it occurred to me that you have been a professor, and that the essays that you've written are permanently interesting. And also that the scholarly side of your work is important – when you begin a project it's often rooted in history or biography.

TK. Well, I am fascinated by history, and by the thing I spoke about at the very beginning, history conveyed through stories and through individual experience, where the personal experience somehow conveys what that historical moment was like. Like the stories my father told us. I'll give you an example of the kind of thing, associated with a place not very far from where we are sitting now. My father was arrested after an ambush near Caltra, and the shooting of a policeman, ironically enough an RIC man, and was put into Galway jail. He became one of the ringleaders of the burning of the jail from the inside and got his name into the *Connaught Tribune*. He always claimed that the signing of the Treaty saved his life, which I think might have been a slight exaggeration. He certainly was very badly beaten in the course of the takeover of the prison afterwards. His account of that, and of the prison itself, encapsulated that whole period of history for me, and the fact that he was telling it as a personal story with himself playing the lead made it even more evocative. And that's the nature of history that fascinates me, the way it yields up stories which you can embellish yourself, because I take great delight in imagining history which in a way contradicts the record. That's the kind of imagination I think I have – an imagination which loves facts but loves them so that they can be changed.

AF. You introduce things that aren't facts, and you challenge the official record – does something like that happen with 'Blake'?

TK. Well, one of the things that's attractive to fiction writers in history are actual gaps in the record, and there is a ten year gap in Blake's biography where we don't know what was going on. He and his wife apparently still worked in their shop in London and produced their extraordinary paintings, but we don't know. That kind of gap in the historical record is immensely attractive to the imagination, because you want to fill it. You can invent a version of the story which would fit into the normal story, and that's what I do in that play. There's no actual record that Blake ever was committed to an asylum, but I invent an asylum for him to be committed into. In that process you can use the historical figure but you can also stretch your own imagination around them, and that's the kind of thing I love doing.

AF. When you are dramatizing things, you make prominent use of the means of production, so that you're more of a modernist than other late-twentieth-century narrative playwrights. Is that fair to say?

TK. What's important is the form of the play – you have to discover the form of the play in the writing. I think that there are many differences between playwriting and other kinds of writing but one difference is spatial. You have to have a spatial sense of what you are doing: you have to know the kind of stage you're going to use. It's in answering technical problems like that that the form of the play finally emerges. And sometimes, I think, in my work there has been a collision between the form that I am using and the material, and for that reason it hasn't worked as well as it should. I find that being open to the question of form is crucial for me. I couldn't function otherwise. So that for that reason the plays do not follow a common identity – each one is stylistically different. *Christ Deliver Us!* is a very loose narrative with short scenes, because that seemed to me to be the style of Wedekind's original and I admire that original immensely. But I had to also account for the kind of 'Irishism' of the material that I was using, so more of that went into that particular form as well.

AF. There's one thing that I can't imagine when I put myself in your shoes as a playwright, and that is the tension that's involved in writing an original play: you have the director, sets are built, actors have rehearsed their lines, opening night is about to happen, and nobody knows yet whether it's going to be good or it's going to be bad. It's a more sudden kind of exposure than in any other art form I can think of.

TK. Well, it's a very unforgiving and a ruthless medium in many respects. It's also immensely rewarding. I'm always shocked on the first day of rehearsal for the first reading of the script by the number of people in the room, and by the fact that these people have gathered to do my work. That's an extraordinary experience, when people with such varied skills are all making a contribution of some kind. I think every playwright has had the experience of absolute disaster – that is simply because the risks involved in putting together something which will work with an immediacy are huge, and the potential for disaster is quite extraordinary. You sometimes see shows where you know that technically this is not a good evening's theatre – but it can be absolutely fascinating for that reason.

AF. I've had the privilege of being able to ask you one question after another all this time. Let's open the session to questions from the audience.

Deirdre Mask. I want to ask a question about your writing process: how do you go about starting a play? Are you one of these people with a very rigorous schedule, or do you write when inspiration strikes you – or a combination of both?

TK. I think that the notion of calling it a process is a bit flattering. I tend to work spasmodically with a great deal of distraction. A play begins for me with a space, and imagining a space, a decorated space. The other side of it is the voice. At the risk of sounding like someone from Lourdes or Knock, I write when I hear voices. For playwriting it's not just a question of hearing a voice in character; you have to hear it at two different levels. You have to hear the voice in character but you also have to hear the actor speaking the voice – and that's the element which makes playwriting actable. It's the element that's missing in the work of all those wonderful writers like Henry James, who tried to write plays and couldn't because they were not listening to the histrionic aspect of speech where they were hearing an actor playing the part. And when you get that, the voice in character and the voice of the actor playing the part, then you can actually put that character into all kinds of situations – it can go on forever. In fact one of the main problems then is to shut the voice up. But if you don't get both the character of the voice and the acting voice, then that character will never live fully on the stage.

Michael D. Higgins. I'd like to ask about the Big House, the importance of the Big House in your writing and to some extent maybe the way that language has become domesticated in the Big House.

TK. Well, I am fascinated by the Anglo-Irish and by the place of the Big House in Irish history, and the role of the Anglo-Irish in our literature. The idea of using an Irish Big House in *The Seagull* wasn't my idea at all; it was the idea of Max Stafford-Clark who was then running the Royal Court Theatre in London. Max's father was a very famous Freudian psychiatrist in Edinburgh, and was employed by John Huston as an advisor on Huston's film of Freud with Montgomery Clift. As a result of that connection, when Max was in Trinity as an undergraduate, Huston invited him down to the house here in County Galway, where Huston was playing the Big House squire to his heart's content. When Max approached me about doing a version of *The Seagull* he knew exactly what he wanted; he wanted to transpose the action into the Anglo-Irish milieu of County Galway, based on his experience of the Huston ménage. Max thought that English language versions of Chekhov gave the impression that the plays were all set in the home counties, and resulted in an English veneer of civility between the audience and the Chekhovian experience, which he felt was much rougher and less genteel (and he's right). So Max had the notion that if it was put into the Irish nineteenth century it would actually bring us closer to Chekhov. So that was how it came about. I had been interested in that phenomenon of the Big House which I explored in *The Big Chapel* as well, simply because it's an intrinsic part of our history: we tend to underestimate the layers of the social that this country has contained, so it's important to kind of connect with that otherness.

Professor Sean Ryder (NUIG). I wanted to ask you a question about the experience of being a playwright as opposed to other forms of writing. It strikes me that it's one of the forms in which there is necessarily a collaborative element. There is a certain point at which you have to release the thing that you have been working on privately to a group of people, as you said earlier. The experience of that must be quite difficult: do you find it enlivening or enriching, or is it also a moment of tension, difficulty and disappointment sometimes, as you see your work taken over by others?

TK. Well, I think that there are playwrights who produce very finished scripts – Brian Friel is one of them – and that's what is given to the group in the theatre. I tend to come into rehearsal in a much less finished fashion, partly because I am trying to figure out whether all these things are going to work. The only way in which you can find out if they are going to work is in the rehearsal room, when an actor starts to work on the thing itself. So I do quite a bit of rewriting during rehearsal. Sometimes they have to stop me and say, 'Go away, and that's it', so I do. I usually spend the first week or ten days in rehearsal and then I leave, because I think it's important that they can bitch about you behind your back and have their own quarrels. Then I come back in at the tail end. So that first week or ten days is very often taken up with rewriting, when I'm discovering that some of this stuff will never work and has to change. I think for that reason that the collaborative quality of theatre is hugely attractive to me – I'm always fascinated by discovering stuff that I didn't know was in the work simply because of the genius of an actor bringing something out, and that's a nice experience. Somebody once said that playwrights are either directors manqué or actors manqué and I think that there is some truth in that. You know, there is the kind of playwright who is directing effects, with that kind of directorial mind, that kind of imagination. Then there is the playwright who is writing speeches for himself which he can't deliver and has to find an actor to do so. So the plays become vehicles for acting.

Dr Lionel Pilkington (NUIG). What are your memories of theatre in Dublin in the 1950s? Were there moves to create a sort of alternative public space?

TK. Well, the curious thing about my memory of theatre in the 50s in Dublin was that you saw more non-Irish theatre than it is possible to do in Dublin today. You had the Pike Theatre and the Dublin Globe Theatre, which Jim Fitzgerald ran with Godfrey Quigley and Norman Rodway. There were a number of significant small theatre companies which were doing very, very good work on non-Irish material, American drama, Lillian Hellman, Tennessee Williams, William Inge, people like that, and European theatre, like Anouilh, Sartre, and Pirandello. We were being exposed to work which was extremely challenging and which was culturally distinct from our own culture, and to that extent theatre was full of surprise and excitement. I was selling tickets when *The Rose Tattoo* was on at the Pike and the theatre was invaded by the police.[2] I came under immense personal pressure to leave the company, and to my shame I did. I was one of a group of people who walked on *The Rose Tattoo*. I went to Alan Simpson and I told him about this pressure that I was under and he said 'Go home', and to my eternal shame I did.

LP. Was that pressure institutional?

TK. I can't go into that, but it was serious. I didn't really recover until I had written *Mr. Roche*. That had an enormous effect on me, the writing of that play. I would never again be bullied by the system. But it also suggests the kind of atmosphere that was in Dublin at that time. I was the auditor of the English Literature Society in UCD and I delivered a paper at the inaugural meeting, on contemporary American fiction. The only problem was that all of the books I discussed were banned. The President of the University at the time who was chairing the meeting was a professor of Classics, a good Galway man called Michael Tierney – a very conservative individual. When he realized I was talking about these banned books he addressed himself to me and said that this was, you know, not the kind of reading that I should be engaged in, that I should be reading decent classical work. And I had read enough of Ovid to be puzzled by that statement. So there was this atmosphere of censorship and pressure in Dublin in the 1950s. I think we all

---

[2] The Pike Theatre was founded in Dublin in 1953 by Alan Simpson and Carolyn Swift. In 1957 Simpson was arrested and imprisoned following a complaint that the Pike production of Tennessee Williams's *The Rose Tattoo* contained 'objectionable passages'. See Roche, *Contemporary Irish Theatre* (1994), p. 40, pp. 70-1 and Christopher Murray, *Twentieth-Century Irish Theatre: Mirror Up To Nation* (Manchester and New York: Manchester University Press, 1997), p. 171.

experienced it to one degree or another. And we all had to find our own way of fighting through it.

National University of Ireland, Galway, 22 March 2011

Gerard Fanning

Tom Kilroy's Big Country

Chuck Connors played Buck Hannassey
'the local trash' in *The Big Country*.

He imagined the village teacher
held a spark for him, or at least

for his character. So when Burl Ives
thought he could then see a way

to resolve the intimacies of water,
he advised his son – the same Buck –

'treat her right, take a bath sometime.'
Misunderstandings of course

but no harm done, since characters
must be allowed space to be foolish,

that is, to take off on their own,
if only to whistle or hop a *sliotar*

off a white-washed wall,
or dream of rustling cattle

across a range of barbed wire
down to The Big Muddy.

So as a match is a battle or a pitch,
or more likely a stage,

let the flight of a ball
or a passing fancy,

summon noisy characters
from the very depths

to audition as they enter
in search of their author.

Notes on Contributors

Gerald Dawe is a poet and Professor of English Literature at Trinity College Dublin. He is a Fellow of the College, Director of the Oscar Wilde Centre for Irish Writing and Director of the M.Phil programme in Creative Writing. He is the author of seven collections of poetry, most recently *Selected Poems* (2012). His other publications include *The Proper Word*, a volume of collected criticism. He has also edited several anthologies of Irish poetry and criticism, including *Earth Voices Whispering: Irish war poetry 1914-1945* (2008).

Peter Fallon is editor and publisher of The Gallery Press which he founded, at the age of 18, in 1970. Recent books include *The Georgics of Virgil* (Oxford World Classics) and *The Company of Horses* (poems). *Peter Fallon: Poet, Publisher, Editor, Translator* (edited by Richard Russell) was published by Irish Academic Press in 2013. In 2012-2013 he held the Burns Library Chair in Irish Studies at Boston College.

Gerard Fanning was born in Dublin in 1952. He is a graduate of UCD. His latest collection is *Hombre: New and Selected Poems* (Dedalus Press, 2011) and in 2013 a selection appeared from Wake Forest University Press.

Adrian Frazier is Director of the MA in Writing and a Professor in the English department at NUI Galway. He is the author of *Behind the Scenes: Yeats, Horniman, and the Struggle for the Abbey Theatre* (1990), *George Moore: 1852-1933* (2000), and *Hollywood Irish: John Ford, Abbey Actors, and the Irish Revival in Hollywood* (2011).

Nicholas Grene is Professor of English Literature at Trinity College Dublin, a Fellow of the College and a Member of the Royal Irish Academy. His books include *The Politics of Irish Drama* (1999), *Shakespeare's Serial History Plays* (2002), *Yeats's Poetic Codes* (2008) and *R.K. Narayan* (2011). His childhood memoir *Nothing Quite Like It* was published in 2011.

Declan Hughes is an award-winning crime novelist and playwright and the co-founder of Dublin's Rough Magic Theatre Company. His plays include *Digging for Fire*, *Twenty Ground*, *Shiver* and *The Last Summer*. He has written five novels, among them *The Wrong Kind of Blood*, *All the Dead Voices* and *City of Lost Girls*.

Christina Hunt Mahony directed graduate studies at the Center for Irish Studies at the Catholic University of America in Washington DC. She is the author of *Contemporary Irish Literature: Transforming Tradition* (1999) and editor of *Out of History: Essays on the Writings of Sebastian Barry* (2006). She has contributed essays on poetry and drama to various volumes on modern Irish literature, and is now Visiting Lecturer in the School of English, Trinity College Dublin.

Wayne Jordan is an Associate Artist of the Abbey Theatre. At the Abbey, he has directed *16 Possible Glimpses*, *No Romance*, *The Plough and the Stars*, *Christ Deliver Us!* and *La Dispute*. He is a graduate of the Samuel Beckett Centre, Trinity College Dublin, is Artistic Director of Randolf SD | The Company and is part of Project Catalyst, an initiative of Project Arts Centre. Most of Wayne's own work has been at Project Arts Centre, where he has directed *Everybody Loves Sylvia*, *Fewer Emergencies*, *The Drowned World*, and *Eeeugh!topia* for his own company. With Thomas Kilroy, Wayne has directed *Christ Deliver Us!*, and a reading of *The Death and Resurrection of Mr. Roche* at the Peacock.

José Lanters is Professor of English and Co-Director of the Center for Celtic Studies at the University of Wisconsin-Milwaukee. Her numerous publications in the field of Irish literature and culture include *Unauthorized Versions: Irish Menippean Satire, 1919-1952* (2000) and *The 'Tinkers' in Irish Literature: Unsettled Subjects and the Construction of Difference* (2008). She has served as Vice-chair for North America of the International Association for the Study of Irish Literatures, and is a past President of the American Conference for Irish Studies.

Marcela Lorca is a Director/Choreographer. She has been Movement Director for the Guthrie Theater since 1991 and is Head of Movement for the University of Minnesota/Guthrie Theater BFA Actor Training Program. Recent directing credits include *The Burial at Thebes*, *The Secret Fall of Constance Wilde*, *The House of The Spirits*, *Three Sisters*,

Blood Wedding, *Wild Honey*, and numerous originally conceived plays that include *Macondo*, *Going Live* and *Time Sensitive*. At the Guthrie she has choreographed over 20 plays and coached movement for over 100 shows. She has worked at many regional theatres in the US as well as the Dominican Republic, Chile, Brazil and Europe. She has also taught at New York University, and the London International School of Performing Arts.

Patrick Mason first joined the Abbey as a director in 1977 and was Artistic Director from 1993 to 1999. His many productions at the Abbey include *The Burial at Thebes*, *The Crucible*, *Observe the Sons of Ulster Marching Towards the Somme*, *The Secret Fall of Constance Wilde*, *By the Bog of Cats* and *Da*. He received a Tony award for Best Director in 1992 for *Dancing at Lughnasa*. His work in opera includes three productions for Wexford Festival, *Don Giovanni* (Dublin Opera), *Don Pasquale* (Opera North, ENO, Israeli Opera), *Rigoletto* (WNO, Opera North) and *Il Trittico* (ENO).

Christopher Murray is Emeritus Professor of English at the School of English, Drama and Film at University College Dublin. He has written on Thomas Kilroy in his *Twentieth-Century Irish Drama: Mirror Up to Nation* (1997), as well as for the special issue of the *Irish University Review* on Kilroy edited by Anthony Roche (2002) and for *The UCD Aesthetic: Celebrating 150 Years of UCD Writers* (2005), also edited by Anthony Roche. *The Theatre of Brian Friel: Tradition and Modernity* was published by Bloomsbury in 2014.

Emer O'Kelly has been drama critic of the *Sunday Independent* since 1992, and writes and broadcasts widely on theatre and the arts in general. She was a newscaster with RTÉ for eighteen years. She was a member of The Arts Council/An Comhairle Ealaíon from 1998-2003, and 2003-2005, and recently completed the second of two five-year terms as a board member of IMMA, the Irish Museum of Modern Art.

Peter O'Rourke is completing his PhD at the University of Leeds, where he is examining the interrelations between performance and spectatorship at the Venice Carnival. Prior to taking up his doctoral studies, Peter was the recipient of the first Friel Scholarship at Queen's University Belfast where he completed a MA in Irish Theatre and Culture. He has published an article on metatheatre in Thomas Kilroy's drama in the journal *Comedy Studies* (2011), and he has taught at the Universities of Hull and Leeds.

Lynne Parker is Artistic Director and co-founder of Rough Magic Theatre Company. Her productions for Rough Magic include *Travesties*, *Peer Gynt*, *Phaedra*, *The Taming of the Shrew*, *Copenhagen*, *Digging for Fire*, *Pentecost*, *Lady Windermere's Fan*, *The Way of the World*, and *Top Girls*. She has won many awards, including *Irish Times* Theatre Awards for Best Director and (four times) for Best Production. Other work includes *The Sanctuary Lamp*, *Down the Line*, *The Drawer Boy* and *Heavenly Bodies* for the Abbey Theatre, and productions for Druid, The Gate, Corn Exchange, Bush Theatre, Almeida, The Old Vic, West Yorkshire Playhouse, RSC, Traverse Theatre, Birmingham Rep, and the Lyric Theatre Belfast. She received the 2008 *Irish Times* Special Tribute Award and was recently awarded an honorary doctorate by Trinity College Dublin.

Kevin Reynolds joined RTÉ as a radio producer in 1995 and has worked across all strands of radio programming in RTÉ Radio from current affairs to arts programming. He is currently the Series Producer of RTÉ Radio Drama. As well as developing new dramatic Irish writing for radio, Kevin has directed plays by Roddy Doyle, Maeve Binchy, Edna O'Brien, Sebastian Barry, Gerard Mannix Flynn, Gary Mitchell, Declan Hughes, Jennifer Johnston, John McGahern and Thomas Kilroy. He has produced new work for radio by Seamus Heaney, Tom Murphy, John Banville, Frank McGuinness and Anne Enright.

Anthony Roche is an Associate Professor in the School of English, Drama and Film at UCD. He was editor of the *Irish University Review* from 1997 to 2002, and edited a special issue of the journal on Thomas Kilroy. Recent publications include *Brian Friel: Theatre and Politics* (2011; paperback, 2012) and *Synge and the Making of Modern Irish Drama* (2013). A revised and updated second edition of *Contemporary Irish Drama*, which includes a chapter on the plays of Thomas Kilroy, was published in 2009.

Michael Scott trained in Paris and has been Theatre Director of Project Arts Centre, Programme Director of the Dublin Theatre Festival and Director of the Tivoli Theatre and RHA Downstairs. Currently Artistic Director of City Theatre Dublin, his productions have been seen in Ireland, Britain, Germany, USA, Iceland and France. Productions include John B. Keane's *The Matchmaker* (Dublin, Edinburgh and New York), *Sisters* with Anna Manahan (Dublin, New York), *The Field*, *The Cuchulain Cycle*, his own plays *Dracula* and *Dancing at the Ballroom of Romance* (City Theatre Dublin), *Bent*, *The Normal Heart* (Project), and Thomas Kilroy's version of *Ghosts* at the Abbey. Currently he is composing a song cycle based on the poetry of W.B. Yeats, *Songs from the Swans at Coole*.

Guy Woodward was awarded a doctorate by Trinity College Dublin in 2012. From 2012-13 he held a Government of Ireland Postdoctoral Fellowship, awarded by the Irish Research Council. He has taught at Trinity, the Institute of Public Administration, Dublin, and the Tecnológico de Monterrey, Mexico. His book, *Culture, Northern Ireland, and the Second World War*, will be published by Oxford University Press in 2015.

Index

A

A.E. see also Russell, George William, 60, 67
Abbey Theatre, xii, 1, 7-8, 18-19, 22, 24-26, 42, 44-45, 61, 66, 72, 75-77, 78-79, 92
Anouilh, Jean, 99
Aristophanes, 42
Artaud, Antonin, 15

B

Bach, Johann Sebastian, 82
Banville, John, 42
Barber, Samuel, 82
BBC, 92, 93
Beckett, Samuel, 15, 25, 27, 29-39, 62, 64
Behan, Brendan, 8, 41
Bergmann, Jesper, 81
Blake, William, 20, 26, 64-65, 86, 95
Blythe, Ernest, 8, 92
Booker Prize, xi, 92
Brecht, Bertolt, 14

C

Callan, Co Kilkenny, 4, 59, 76, 89-90, 93
Carr, Marina, 41
Catholic Church, 3, 10, 18, 22, 86, 91
Channel 4, 94
Chekhov, Anton, 3, 8, 14, 24, 42, 45, 66-67, 97
Cusack, Cyril, 34, 92

D

Dante Alighieri, 38
de Valera, Éamon, 3, 16
Deane, Seamus, 94
Dostoevsky, Fyodor, 17-18
Dublin Globe Theatre, 99
Dublin Theatre Festival, 16, 21-22, 84, 92

E

Edwards, Hilton, 9

F

Faber and Faber, 44

Field Day Theatre Company, 9, 21, 24-26, 44, 94
Fitzgerald, Jim, 92, 99
Freud, Sigmund, 61, 80-81, 97
Friel, Brian, 8, 9, 22-25, 41, 44-45, 63, 65-66, 73, 93-94, 98

G

Gaiety Theatre, 34
German Expressionism, 11
Giacometti, Alberto, 27

H

Heaney, Seamus, 73, 94
Hepburn, Doreen, 84-85
HIV, 83-85
Huston, John, 97

I

Ibsen, Henrik, 3, 14, 26, 37, 42, 45, 68-69, 85
  Ghosts, 45, 69
Inge, William, 99

J

James, William, 80
Johnston, Denis, 12, 24, 63
Joyce, James, 8, 60, 80

K

Keane, John B., 43
Kearney, Richard, 62
Kelly, David, 84-85
Kennelly, Brendan, 42
Kilroy, Thomas
  Big Chapel, The, xi, 5, 59-60, 72, 89-90, 92, 98
  'Blake', 1, 20, 49-57, 64-65, 70, 75, 86, 95
  Christ Deliver Us!, ix, 3-4, 9, 18-19, 24, 45, 68, 70-72, 75-77, 90, 96
  Double Cross, 3, 4-5, 9, 12, 18, 21, 24-25, 44, 63, 70
  Ghosts, 3, 5, 45, 67, 68-69, 83-86
  'Groundwork for an Irish Theatre', 2, 8, 73, 75
  Henry, 69-70
  In the Garden of the Asylum, xi, 63, 80-82
  Madame MacAdam Travelling Theatre, The, 1, 3, 9, 18, 25, 45, 66, 70, 94
  My Scandalous Life, 14, 45
  O'Neill, The, 8-11, 18, 20, 22, 44, 65, 92
  Seagull, The, 8, 24, 45, 66-68, 93, 97
  Secret Fall of Constance Wilde, The, 8, 13-14, 20, 26-27, 43, 45, 60, 65, 66, 70, 82-83
  Shape of Metal, The, 26, 27, 41, 45, 64-65, 72, 77-79
  Six Characters in Search of an Author, 8, 69
  Tea and Sex and Shakespeare, 3, 22-23, 44, 61, 63-67, 73

Kleist, Heinrich von, 42

L

Leonard, Hugh, 8, 65
Littlewood, Joan, 8
Lodge, David, 60
Lorca, Federico García, 82

M

Mac Anna, Tomás, 8, 92
Magdalene Laundries, 71
Magee, Heno, 43
Mahon, Derek, 60
Mamet, David, 66
Mason, Patrick, xi, 1, 11, 26, 43, 75, 86-87
McCabe, Eugene, 8, 41, 43
McCann, Donal, 22
Milton, John, 38
Molière, 42
Moore, George, 59-60
Murphy, Tom, 8, 41-43, 63, 73, 93

N

Ní Chuilleanáin, Eiléan, 42
Nietzsche, Friedrich, 17-18
Nolan, Christopher, 84
Nolan, Jim, 26, 41

O

Olympia Theatre, 92
Osborne, John, 8

P

Parker, Lynne, 3-4, 75, 77-80
Parker, Stewart, 41
Peacock Theatre, 11, 21, 22, 36, 42, 86
Pike Theatre, 99
Pinter, Harold, 45, 72
Pirandello, Luigi, 3, 8, 14, 42, 45, 67, 69-70, 99
Project Theatre, 42, 61

Q

Quigley, Godfrey, 92, 99

R

Racine, Jean, 35, 42
Rea, Stephen, 12, 24, 94
Rilke, Rainer Maria, 17-18
Robinson, Mary, 69
Rodway, Norman, 99
Rostand, Edmond, 42
Rough Magic Theatre Company, 60-61
Royal Court Theatre, 8, 22, 65, 97
RTÉ, 11, 12, 80-81
Russell, George William
 see A.E.
Ryan Report, 71

S

Sartre, Jean-Paul, 99
Scott, Michael, 3, 75, 83-86
Second World War, 3, 12, 18, 24-25, 93
Shakespeare, William, 22, 25, 69, 76
Shaw, George Bernard, 29-39
Smith, Brendan, 92
Sophocles, 42
St Kieran's College, Kilkenny, 90-91
Stafford-Clark, Max, 22, 97
Strindberg, August, 14
Synge, J.M., 7-8, 20, 28, 34, 62

T

Tóibín, Colm, 60
Tóibín, Niall, 92
Trinity College Dublin, xi, xii, 1, 9, 22, 28, 41- 42
Turgenev, Ivan, 42

U

University College Dublin (UCD), 23, 59, 80, 90-92, 99

W

Wedekind, Frank, 3, 8, 18-19, 24, 42, 45, 67, 68, 70-72, 96
  Spring Awakening, 3, 8, 18-19, 24, 67, 70-71, 76

Wesker, Arnold, 8
Whitaker, T.K., 15
Wilde, Oscar, 5, 13-14, 26-27, 60, 65-66, 80, 82-83
Williams, Tennessee, 73, 99

Y

Yeats, W.B, 13-15, 26, 29-30, 32, 34-38, 67

www.ingramcontent.com/pod-product-compliance
Lightning Source LLC
Chambersburg PA
CBHW051102230426
43667CB00013B/2416